The Way of the W... ...ugh Travel
"...illuminates the soul and spirit of traveling in a way that is poignant, sometimes amusing, and always wise."
—The Bloomsbury Review

The Road Within: True Stories of Transformation and the Soul
"Remarkable writers chronicle remarkable inner experiences from every corner of the world...entrancing, filled with wonder... radiant expansions of what it is to be human."
—NAPRA Review

A Woman's Path: Women's Best Spiritual Travel Writing
"A sensitive exploration of women's lives that have been unexpectedly and spiritually touched by travel experiences...highly recommended."
—Library Journal

The Ultimate Journey: Inspiring Stories of Living and Dying
"A glorious collection of writings about the ultimate adventure. A book to keep by one's bedside—and close to one's heart."
—Philip Zaleski, editor, The Best Spiritual Writing series

Pilgrimage: Adventures of the Spirit
"This magnificent collection should be found at the crossroads of every seeker's soul."
—Steve Zikman, author of The Power of Travel

The Sword of Heaven
"A very beautiful book. The story has an intensity and inwardness that is moving to me."
—Robert Bly, poet and author of Iron John

365 Travel: A Daily Book of Journeys, Meditations, and Adventures
"Armchair travelers, backpackers, luxury travelers, and adventurers alike will 'get taken in' by Bach's well-chosen and varied selections."
—ForeWord Magazine

TRAVELERS' TALES BOOKS

Country and Regional Guides
America, Australia, Brazil, Central America, Cuba, France, Greece,
India, Ireland, Italy, Japan, Mexico, Nepal, Spain, Thailand;
American Southwest, Grand Canyon, Hawai'i,
Hong Kong, Paris, San Francisco, Tuscany

Women's Travel
Her Fork in the Road, A Woman's Path, A Woman's
Passion for Travel, A Woman's World, Women in the Wild,
A Mother's World, Safety and Security for Women
Who Travel, Gutsy Women, Gutsy Mamas

Body & Soul
The Spiritual Gifts of Travel, The Road Within,
Love & Romance, Food, The Fearless Diner, The Adventure
of Food, The Ultimate Journey, Pilgrimage

Special Interest
Not So Funny When It Happened,
The Gift of Rivers, Shitting Pretty, Testosterone Planet,
Danger!, The Fearless Shopper, The Penny Pincher's
Passport to Luxury Travel, The Gift of Birds, Family Travel,
A Dog's World, There's No Toilet Paper on the Road Less
Traveled, The Gift of Travel, 365 Travel

Footsteps
Kite Strings of the Southern Cross, The Sword of Heaven,
Storm, Take Me With You, Last Trout in Venice, The Way of the
Wanderer, One Year Off, The Fire Never Dies

Classics
The Royal Road to Romance,
Unbeaten Tracks in Japan, The Rivers Ran East

The Spiritual Gifts of Travel

THE BEST OF TRAVELERS' TALES

The Spiritual
Gifts of Travel

THE BEST OF TRAVELERS' TALES

Edited by

JAMES O'REILLY AND

SEAN O'REILLY

TRAVELERS' TALES

SAN FRANCISCO

Art Direction: Michele Wetherbee
Interior design: Kathryn Heflin and Susan Bailey
Cover photograph: Lamaist scripture on stone, Tibet © Image Bank; Monk © Tsuyoshi
Kindaichi/Photonica
Mandala Illustrations: Alexandria Brady
Page layout: Cynthia Lamb, using the fonts Bembo and Remedy

Distributed by: Publishers Group West, 1700 Fourth Street, Berkeley, California
94710.

Library of Congress Cataloguing-in-Publication Data

The spiritual gifts of travel : the best of Travelers' Tales / edited by James O'Reilly and
Sean O'Reilly. — 1st ed.
     p. cm.
   Includes bibliographical references
   ISBN 1-885211-69-4 (alk.paper)
    1. Travel—Anecdotes. 2. Travelers—Anecdotes. 3. Travelers' writings. I. O'Reilly,
James, 1953- II. O'Reilly, Sean. III. Travelers' Tales (Firm)

G151 .S66 2002
910—dc21

                                                                    2002017359

                                   First Edition
                           Printed in the United States
                             10 9 8 7 6 5 4 3 2

I went looking for adventure and romance, and so I found them…but I found also something I had never expected. I found a new self.

—SOMERSET MAUGHAM

Table of Contents

Part Two
HEALING

Part Three
MYSTERY

The Spiritual Gifts of Travel:
An Introduction

Spirituality and travel have been linked from the beginning of human history. The oldest spiritual quest that we have an inkling of is ancient man's quest for the *House of the Sun*. One can imagine our ancestors seeking this house where the sun must surely have set. How many unsung voyages since that time have been inspired by the setting sun and its ancient choir of steepled light? The eye is drawn relentlessly towards the rising and setting sun, and where the eye wanders with hope and imagination, there goes the soul. It is perhaps no accident that monks and holy men and women of all religions have gone on pilgrimage and journeys of knowledge since the beginning of recorded history.

Buddhism spread from Nepal and India in the third century B.C., at roughly the same time that Alexander the Great surged to the East in the hope of finding the ends of the earth. Who knows what gods or demons drove Alexander? We do know, however, that he was a pupil of Aristotle and that the God Aristotle preached was a God of perfection who drew all things to himself. Alexander sought this perfection on the road of conquest and discovery. Hundreds of years later, Christianity spread throughout the Greco Roman Empire with the injunction to go and teach all nations. Five centuries later Islam rose and spread its message through the ghost footpaths of that same empire. They were all travelers in search of spiritual booty and adventure. They still are.

We don't often think of the great religions as being promoters of travel but history teaches us that the beginnings of the tourist industry, as we know it today, has its roots in the impulse to make pilgrimage to holy sites, and in the ancient urge that is written into our genes to go forth and explore both the inner and outer terrain of the universe into which we've been born.

So where does this leave us today? At the dawn of the twenty-first century, we find ourselves in the paradoxical position of being afraid to travel precisely because the religious impulse and the desire to travel are in fact inextricably linked, and in many instances, in conflict, from the Balkans to Israel, Sri Lanka to Tibet, Kashmir to Nigeria, Afghanistan to Saudi Arabia, Northern Ireland to Iran. The ancient quest to find the House of the Sun, a metaphor for the search for light, must be reinvested with modern thinking and aspirations. Travel and the right to travel, to move freely as one wishes, goes beyond national boundaries and forms the framework of what might be declared a universal human right. Our notions of national boundaries have come under increased pressure as millions of people seek a better life in countries that promise opportunity or freedom from oppression. Travel has become the metaphor of freedom. It is no accident then that those who oppose freedom seek to restrict travel. One has only to think of the Berlin Wall or the former Soviet Union, which wouldn't allow maps to be sold in the open market for fear of where its citizens might have wandered or wanted to wander, to the travel restrictions that many governments put on their rural populations.

The spiritual gifts of travel are legion. Who is not made better, humbled, or enlightened by a visit to countries not of their own origin? Whose consciousness is not augmented by hearing the hopes and fears of people raised in foreign cultures? Who cannot learn from the spiritual practices of religions other than their own?

The Spiritual Gifts of Travel seeks to uncover some of the common spiritual pathways that are discovered when human beings approach experience without judgement or prejudice. Travel can take us out of the deadly grip of habit and the narrow focus of culture and cast us upon the great road of spirituality–sometimes whether we wish it or not. Somerset Maugham put it beautifully:

> I went looking for adventure and romance, and so I found them…but I found also something I had never expected. I found a new self.

Come with us and walk the road of self-discovery: We've gathered here some of our favorite stories of travel and transformation which have appeared in our destination anthologies, thematic anthologies, and other books we've published. Kim Chernin, raised in a family of Marxists, discovers spirituality on her knees one winter in rural Ireland. Englishman David Yeadon encounters an old Native American sage on the back roads of Oregon and continues on an irrevocably changed man. Alison Wright has her heart split open while working in one of Mother Theresa's Calcutta clinics; Leo Banks encounters the deep mystery of the American Southwest in a burning glove by the side of the road. David Abram is stripped naked by the gaze of a condor in the Himalayas, and Dennis Covington encounters a strange and lovely madness in snake worship in Alabama. Laurie Gough encounters the undead on the beaches of a Greek island and Mikkel Aaland is given a quest by a Shinto priest in Japan that takes him all over the world.

Like the story of Saint Paul on the road to Damascus, these sudden encounters are all shaped by a hidden light. They are but a few of the remarkable experiences you will read about in

The Spiritual Gifts of Travel. Adventure and transformation await. Let us seek, as does Richard Halliburton in his story, "The Garden of Immortality," our own place in the House of the Sun.

—SEAN O'REILLY AND JAMES O'REILLY

PART ONE

IGNITION

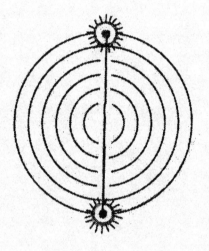

KIM CHERNIN

✦

Awakening the Stone

Was everything she'd been told
about the universe wrong?

I RECALL A WINTER DAY LONG AGO. I WAS LIVING IN IRELAND. I had driven from Dublin up into the mountains, feeling depressed and despondent. I took no pleasure in my studies, was bored and restless during serious conversations with my friends.

Looking back, I recognize this urgent dissatisfaction as the beginning of initiation. It is a time of dislocation. One grows tired of one's favorite food, can't sleep at night, gives up on the books and music one loves best, loses interest in even the oldest and most loyal obsessions, stands up suddenly in the midst of conversations, walks about by oneself, writes down scraps of thought on scraps of paper, looks for counsel in familiar places, hears nothing worth listening to, frowns, alienates friends, eats too much or stops eating much at all, feels dreadfully tired and sick of it all and at the same time as if one were in a state of unbearable suspense, waiting for the phone to ring, for the mail to arrive, for that stranger to walk around the

3

corner. And meanwhile nothing happens and everything is just about to happen and you are, you think, too old for this sort of thing and then the despondency starts to grow and the anxiety becomes more acute and you know you're up against it, whatever it is. You can't turn back. Have you gone forward? You can't go forward. Where is there to go?

It was a cold day, I remember clearly. There was frost on the ground. Up in the mountains the trees were covered with a thin coating of ice. I was on my way to a spot my friends and I visited frequently, where we would go for picnics and drink stout and wrap ourselves in blankets and shiver, even in summer, in the cold. To get there, we had always driven past the Powerscourt Estate, but we had never stopped to visit. This time I stopped. I pulled over to the right and got out of the car, stamping my feet, slapping my hands against my thighs.

An old man came out of the gatehouse; he was surprised to see me, touched his finger to his cap, showed me the bell on the gate. A scrappy dog growled and came toward me, tugging at his rope. I had several cookies in my pocket. I threw one to him. He jumped up and caught it in the air, his stump of a tail wagging furiously. The gate swung back a few feet; I walked through and turned to wave at the old man, who locked it behind me.

So there I was, a visitor to the Powerscourt Estate, locked in until I rang the bell and threw cookies to the dog to make my way out again. Well, why not? This is why not. From the moment the old man disappeared into the gatehouse again I felt a panic of loneliness, as if I'd been left alone in a world of strangers. I wanted to run back to the car and head out for Dublin, but I was ashamed to face the old man again.

The road was smooth and level; it was kept free of rocks and ran along a slight incline on which trees were densely planted. Their leaves had turned yellow but had not dropped from the branches. They seemed strange and otherworldly, but I kept looking at them with a childlike curiosity. Whenever the breeze rose the leaves chimed together and made a desolate, frozen rattle.

Then, from out of my panic and despondency, there came an odd sensation. I felt as if I were a small girl, with little hands and legs. My entire body surged with delight, as if it had just discovered the pleasure of being a body. I jumped a fallen tree, climbed a rock, leaped down again, ran on. Soon, I came upon a flock of black sheep, grazing below me near a cluster of trees. There was not a single white sheep among them. All around me the colors were growing deeper and richer, the air was saturated with light. The flock of black sheep seemed to be grazing joyfully upon a grass so vibrant I could scarcely believe it was a material substance. Then I noticed the gray stones scattered about here and there in the field; they, too, were vibrating and pulsing with the same kind of intensity. "They're alive," I gasped. Nature, which I'd always imagined a brute dead stuff, had some kind of vivid life to it.

I had by then reached the valley's farthest edge. With every step I took, I was intending to go back. There was something uncanny in the place, bringing out something weird in me. I did not want to think that stones were alive. I did not want the logical categories through which I ordered the world to break down and desert me. I was addicted to what I then called rationality—to holding the world view the men of my time thought most plausible. Humans had consciousness and spirit and feelings. Trees and stones and sheep did not. I wanted to get out of anyplace that was teaching me anything else.

But then I noticed a waterfall pouring down a steep rock face that dropped precipitously into the river, and I was running toward it. Below me was a rock pool, churning and

foaming with a peculiar gleefulness. I stood there laughing
back at it and then, all at once, I had the strong desire to
throw off my clothes and immerse myself in the pool. I
looked around me. The valley was deserted. The sheep grazed
quietly; from the distance I heard the rattle from the frozen
leaves. "Do it, do it," something in me kept urging, from a
child's sense of delight in what should not be done. But who
had decided what was and was not permitted? Here I was, a
woman of the twentieth century, capable of making my own
way in the world, presumably liberated, but in reality chained
by unquestioned assumptions about the way thinking was to
take place and the world was to be experienced and I, myself,
was to behave.

I turned back toward the valley. Light was pouring down
over the black sheep and the green fields as if someone has
just lifted a bucket and were watering everything in sight. I
looked up and saw that this light was flooding down from a
sky that was not any longer a sky. It was, as I looked, with-
drawing behind shimmering veils of blue light. And now the
whole valley became one great wave of light, rising and
falling, shaping and dissolving. My idea that the sky was a sky
and the tree a tree, separate and distinguishable from one another, had to be questioned. Here they were dissolving into
one another. Was it possible everything I had been told about
the universe was simply an assumption, a style of perception,
rather than truth?

It was too late to flee from the place. I, the rationalist, was
in the grip of extreme emotion. I could fight it off, run away,
or surrender and find out what it meant. I found myself before
an immense tree. Near the bottom it had been split almost in
two by lightning and in the charred, concave base, a brilliant
green-and-yellow lichen was growing. I stared at the tree, a
natural altar. I wondered, had the Druids worshipped this

tree? I tried to distract myself with this thought and meanwhile my body was doing something peculiar. I noticed it, thought I should fight it, was doing it anyway. Then it was done. There I was, on the ground in front of the tree. Tears streaming down my face. I, raised in a family of Marxist atheists, down on my knees, worshipping?

Kim Chernin is a novelist, poet, and the author of several nonfiction books, including The Hungry Self, The Woman Who Gave Birth to Her Mother, In My Mother's House, *and* Reinventing Eve: Modern Woman in Search of Herself, *from which this story was excerpted. Chernin lives in the San Francisco Bay Area, where she is a psychoanalyst in private practice.*

DAVID YEADON

We Shall Live Again

Ancient wisdom resides around each bend in the road.

DEEP IN THE MOUNTAINS OF OREGON, WAY BACK IN THE Klamath Ranges, I'd journeyed on back roads so faint and occasionally nonexistent that I wondered if I'd ever find my way out again. I wasn't exactly lost. Or maybe I was. Maybe I wanted to be lost, to be utterly vulnerable, to be open to whatever came along, to test my faith in fate once again.

And what came along was quite remarkable.

He was an old Indian. No, not a "Native American." He laughed at such PC phraseology. "White man's guilt," he called it and chuckled behind broken teeth. His face was deep mahogany-brown, his skin as wrinkled and weathered and tough as rhino hide, and his smile bright enough to illuminate a football stadium.

It was the smile that made me stop the camper and walk over to meet him. He was sitting near the side of the track on a large boulder, dressed in worn jeans, a big woolen sweater, and a purple bandanna over which his gray, wiry hair fell guru-like in matted tresses down to his shoulder blades.

I think I saw his smile before I really saw him. Maybe a trickle of sunlight caught his teeth. Who knows. But first came that great grin and then came Bill.

Bill! I was disappointed by his name, hoping for Eagle-Rising or Catch-Bear-for-Breakfast or Coyote-Calling or something a bit more Indianlike. But Bill it was and Bill it remained. He said he was some subtribe of Cherokee I'd never heard of. He pointed up through the trees to a cabin perched high atop a rock outcrop on the ridgeline of the mountain. He asked if I was thirsty. I wasn't but I said I was, so he led the way slowly up through the thick undergrowth between towering pines to his lonely aerie.

The vistas were incredible. All the way south down endless serrated ranges. The receding lines of hills blurred into warm blue mists. Two bald eagles soared on spirals, barely moving their wings—just gliding in great upward circles of flight.

He offered me water and then boiled up some concoction on an outdoor stove. He called it "tea" but it was unlike any tea I've ever drunk before or since. At first it seemed insipid—rather like the barely flavored hot water you get in the more mediocre of Chinese restaurants. But as I continued to sip from the mug slowly, watching the eagles, enjoying the amazing views and peering down into shadowy valleys and canyons, something began to work its magic. I felt increasingly thirsty and the more I drank of the tea the more its flavor expanded into a spectral array of tastes, from the tartest of lemons to the sweetest of sweets I've ever experienced. Its aroma was of lavender, rose petals, and peaches; its taste was more complex but somewhere in the mix seemed raisins, oranges, honey, and mint. The rest was indefinable. But it was wonderful and I felt wonderful and Bill just sat there sipping and grinning and grinning and sipping.

Our silence was full of fellowship. It seemed to go on for

hours. No talk. Just tea-sipping and gazing. No mind-yammer either for a change. Just each moment. Perfect, whole, and complete in itself.

Eventually there was conversation of a kind. He talked of the mountains, of a tribal powwow he'd attended (no whites invited) a week or so ago, of the songs and the chantings that had stretched on through whole days and nights.

I asked him if he could sing one or two of the songs. He grinned as if he knew that's precisely what I'd ask and began by beating a stick in the dust at his feet, making a soft puckering kind of sound like distant drums, drums heard far away somewhere deep in the heart of the forest.

The sound and rhythm were hypnotic. At first it was a simple beat but as he continued it seemed to develop subtle counter-rhythms and a backbeat and the foot-shuffle hiss of flesh on soft sand (with my eyes closed it really sounded like scores of feet, all shuffle-dancing together).

And slowly he began to sing. Long plaintive lines, initially minor variations on a drone, in a deep monotone, but gradually expanding into higher registers, becoming plaintive, then stern and proud, then whispery, then sadly plaintive again as if beseeching something, asking for some special favor, for grace and generosity from...what?...the power of the earth, the sky? I wasn't sure. At least, not until much later.

But it was enough just to listen without having to "understand." Bill's face was lifted up toward the sun. The golden light of early evening etched the leathery puckers of his cheeks and gave the creases deep glowing shadows. His eyes were closed. Sometimes he was grinning, exuding utter happiness. Other times, in the softer plaintive passages, his face was devoid of expression as if he were opening himself up wide to receive whatever favors were to be bestowed upon him.

The faintest of breezes blew across the ridge, nudging fallen leaves and cooling us as we sat together, me with my tea and Bill with his songs and his tapping stick. And if I listened, really listened, I could hear the echoes of other voices, voices in unison, in a kind of earthy harmony, a harmony resonant with the earth and all the mysteries and powers and wonders contained within the earth.

Later, much later, I asked Bill if he could tell me what one of the songs meant—a particularly beautiful song with a fluid melodic line and a note at the end of some of the lines that was like no other note I'd ever heard—a quartertone, like the songs I'd heard so often in Iran? Or something else, a note not capable of placement on a page of written music. It was eerie and beautiful and seemed to have the ability to hang almost tangibly in the air long after he had moved on to other song lines.

"The words are simple," he said and grinned and I knew he didn't believe that at all. And I knew that they expressed the soul and spirit of ancient cultures, now almost destroyed and lost. And I knew—just by the sound of the music and those elusive grace notes—that they reflected a total, all-encompassing understanding of the way of all life—of a world in which man exists in harmony with all living and inanimate things and is part of the natural timeless rhythm which shapes and nurtures his environment and his whole existence. These songs were not contrived for idle amusement and entertainment, neither were they sung for the benefit of a few discerning listeners. For thousands upon thousands of years (just pause and think of that, particularly in relation to our own neophyte American culture barely a couple of centuries old) they were part of the tribal fabric, the melding force of ancient peoples, full of meaning, power, and deep spiritual resonance—direct communications with the infinite.

I was an eager student and I think Bill could sense that. I asked him to tell me the words of some of his songs. He smiled, nodded as if he knew I'd ask that too and began with the shortest of songs—the haiku-like "Eagle's Song" (three simple lines, repeated and repeated):

> The sun's rays
> Lie along my wings
> And stretch beyond their tips

Then he again sang the "Corn Song":

> The corn grows up
> The waters of the dark clouds drop, drop.
> The rain descends.
> The waters from the corn leaves drop, drop.
> The rain descends.
> The waters from the plains, drop, drop.
> The corn grows up.
> The waters of the dark mists drop, drop.

And then "The Rock":

> Unmoved
> From time without end,
> You rest in the midst of the coming winds,
> In the winds
> You rest, aged one.
> Small grasses grow around you
> You are covered with the droppings of the birds,
> Your top decked with downy feathers.
> Oh, aged one.

Then another short haiku:

> I am simply on the earth
> Need I be afraid?

And then the most beautiful song of all, "The Mountain Chant," the one with those strange plaintive notes:

> In beauty may I walk.
> All day long may I walk.
> Through the returning seasons may I walk.
> On the trail marked with pollen may I walk.
> With grasshoppers about my feet may I walk.
> With dew about my feet may I walk.
> With beauty may I walk.

And finally he sang the most powerful short-song of all again, chanted endlessly—"The Ghost Dance":

> We shall live again.
> We shall live again.

Evening was creeping in quickly now over the purpling ridges and I realized that I had to find my way out of the mountains on that elusive back road before dark.

I thanked Bill for his kindness and his company and then asked a question that I hadn't intended to ask. It just sort of appeared: "That last song. 'The Ghost Dance.' 'We shall live again.' Do you really believe that?"

Once again that grin. All-enveloping. All-embracing. "Yes," Bill replied simply, grinning that grin.

"But how?" I asked. "When so few Indians—so few of you—are left?"

Bill didn't respond to that one. He just grinned wider than ever—looked right into my eyes, deeper, deeper than anyone had looked before, and something inside me suddenly opened up—like a box, long locked and now unlocked. And I felt—I truly felt—as if he'd placed not only all the songs he'd sung for me into that box but the spirit behind the songs, the oh-so-ancient, oh-so-timeless knowledge that gave those songs their all-encompassing life and power.

And as I walked down the path from his tiny ridge-top cabin I felt myself filled with enormous richness and energy and vitality and the words of the "Ghost Dance" seemed to surround me and permeate every particle of my being. I heard the words as clearly as if Bill were singing them beside me. And I heard something else. I heard Bill's voice inside me saying, "We shall live again.... We shall live again."

And I knew how too.

A native of Yorkshire, England, David Yeadon has worked as an author, illustrator, journalist, and photographer for more than twenty-five years. He is the author of numerous books including, The Back of Beyond, Lost Worlds, *and* The Way of the Wanderer, *from which this was excerpted. He is also a regular travel correspondent for* National Geographic, National Geographic Traveler, The Washington Post, *and* The New York Times. *Currently, he writes the "Hidden America" column for* National Geographic Traveler. *In between travel odysseys he lives with his wife, Anne, in Japan, where she is a Professor in Vision Rehabilitation, and also in a Hudson Valley lakeside house, north of Manhattan.*

✶ ✶ ✶

Bola's Gift

Truth splits the heart wide open.

BOLA WAS THE MOST HIDEOUSLY DEFORMED MAN I HAD EVER seen in my life. Yet, even here in Calcutta, someone had loved him enough to keep him alive for twenty-three years. I was living in Nepal working as a photographer for UNICEF, Save the Children, and various other aid organizations. Over the years I had become overwhelmed by the devastation I was seeing through the lens of my camera and wanted to relate with people on a more intimate level once again. This is how I found myself working at Mother Teresa's orphanage in India.

The children at the orphanage were doe-eyed beauties in desperate need of love and attention, much like many of the other children I had been photographing throughout Asia. Frustrated nurses brusquely pinched the children's noses while trying to shove food into their mouths. One baby I held was so small I was able to cup him in the palm of my hand. His brown wrinkled skin sagged around his tiny malnourished ankles. Another baby giggled uncontrollably as I threw him into the air. "Hold that beautiful smile, you" I thought. Covered in scabs and warts, this little cherub hadn't yet realized his fate as an orphan in Calcutta.

On Easter Sunday, Mother Teresa came to visit the orphanage and attend mass. It was hard to believe that this small shrunken woman from Albania, a face full of wrinkles, had become such a prominent symbol of all that is good in the world. Gliding into the room, she gave me a blessing and a small silver medallion of Mother Mary to wear around my neck. With a knowing smile she encouraged me to see her home of the destitute and dying. Just to visit.

The next day I hired a rickshaw to take me across town. Dripping with sweat, the rickshaw driver dropped me in front of an unpretentious building next to a bathing ghat. Working my way around through the throng of people I stopped at the Kali Temple. Tended by a widowed priestess, women were tying stones and praying to a fruitless cactus tree covered with china roses in the hopes of becoming fertile. "This is a fertility tree," a woman explained to me. "We come to pray here when we have trouble giving birth." I wondered if their suffering must be part of the sacrifice. Ironically, this was right next to Kali Ghat, Mother Teresa's Home for the Destitute and Dying, where people can come and die with dignity.

And dying they were. The street was lined with the sick and elderly waiting to get inside. I nearly gagged from the strong smell of antiseptic as I entered the building. I was immediately greeted with the sight of a nun carving the dead flesh away from a leper's foot. Dressed in flowing white robes, with blue trim, one of the nuns guided me to the women's area in the back of the building. The scene seemed as if from a concentration camp. Half-naked women with shaved heads ran from the staff and volunteers who tried to bathe them, while other patients rocked back and forth on the beds, mumbling incoherently. One woman with an open robe, exposed the fat, flesh, and bone gaping from an exposed wound on her backside. I felt ashamed by my recoil.

We continued through the room and into the men's area. Again, the smell of pungent antiseptic was overpowering. Men stared at me intently from their rows of green cots with the unmistakable sounds of hacking tuberculosis and vomiting. Still, I felt relieved to be away from the screeching women. There was one more bed in the corner to pass before I was finally free to head back out the door and into the chaos and sunshine. A gray-haired old man, who introduced himself as Andy O'Connor from Ireland, was trying to feed a much younger Indian man lying on the cot. Andy introduced him as Bola, "strong one." "He's gotten this far," Andy explained. Bola heard his name and craned his closely shaved head on the pillow to look at me. His eyes were soulful, yet imprisoned in a repulsive body, which was now flat as a Frisbee, from years of lying on a bed. His thin matchstick bones were abnormally twisted and misshapen.

"He seems taken with you," said Andy. "Why don't you try to feed him?"

This was more than I had bargained for. I was, after all, only touring the place. I wanted to return to cuddling children, not to confront illness and death to such an uncomfortable degree. Then I remembered that this was actually what my pilgrimage was about. Human connection without a camera. Globs of the pasty cereal were already dribbling from the sides of his mouth as I scooped up a spoonful of the gray gruel and tried to work it through his partially opened lips. Surprisingly, he managed to keep it down. Then another and another. Andy was amazed.

"We've been trying to feed him for days, and this is the first time he's actually been eating," said Andy incredulously. "He thinks you're an angel." Sure enough, Bola hadn't stopped staring at me since I began feeding him. "Will you please come back tomorrow? No one else has been able to get any food into him. We've been afraid that he won't make it."

And so I returned every day for the next six weeks.

Every morning I made my way through the markets in search of the ripest oranges to squeeze to make juice for Bola. I found bananas, which I mashed to a pulp. I bought Cadbury's chocolate bars, the Indian kind, made of wax, so they wouldn't melt in the heat. I crushed them down to a fine powder and fed them to Bola when the nurses weren't looking. The treats I brought became our secret. Unable to speak, the love pouring from his eyes spoke volumes. I wondered about the people in his life who had loved him enough to take care of him this long in such a drastically poor country, and then left him here to die. No one knew anything about his past. He was left at the doorstep like so many others.

One day I came in and Andy asked me to help him bathe a little boy who was in the bed next to Bola. We had nick-named him Toro, "small one." I had tried to feed him, but it was no use. His skin was peeling away from malnutrition and he had a hacking bloody cough from tuberculosis. He was so ill that layers of his skin came away as Andy and I pulled off the bandages. My heart broke, as I held his bony body in my arms, trying to absorb his pain into my own. With barely the strength to wince, he put his head on my lap and whimpered. "Poor thing, he just wants a mum to hold him," said Andy. I stayed late with him, praying for him to die. But his will was so strong. Suddenly, I heard the rattle of death gurgling in his small chest. His eyes gave me a last look before they rolled back into his head and I felt his body go limp. That tiny bit of life in my arms was now free as a bird. "What an honor," said Andy. "He chose you to help him die." I should have been exuberant, but I felt overwhelmed with sadness.

I frantically looked around for a nurse, but they were all too busy to deal with this common occurrence. I thought about Andy's words. This was my responsibility. I wrapped Toro's small body in the still warm sheet, using a pin from my camera bag to close it up. Andy helped me carry him the short distance down the road to the Ganges River. We said a small prayer and dropped the body into the water.

Death is such a part of life in India. I tried to imagine dropping a body into the river in New York City, with hundreds of people watching. We walked back to the Kali Ghat home and made our way to the roof. I looked down at the senseless confusion of people below us. There was a continuous line of people waiting to get into the home. Vacancy by death only. It seemed neverending. The crush of people didn't seem jostling and exciting to me anymore. It seemed pathetic. "I just don't get it," I whispered and began to weep.

Andy put his arm around me. "You know, my wife died ten years ago. She was the sweetest woman in the world and loved me immensely, but I took her for granted. I was working as a very successful architect in Dublin. I was a philanderer and it hurt my wife greatly. One day she came home and told me that she had been diagnosed with cancer. Ironically, I had to have a triple bypass at the time, and we spent four months in the hospital together. We grew so close during that time, and it wasn't until then that I really appreciated her. She died the day I left the hospital." Andy had learned his life lessons harshly.

"After her death I gave up my job, and came here to work at Mother Teresa's full time, hoping to redeem myself. I've been here for five years. I still don't have any answers. In my room I have statues of Buddha, Ganesh, and Christ. Who knows what happens to us when we die, but I want to be sure to have my bases covered," he said with a chuckle. "All I know is, one person can't save the world. But if you touch just one person then that's something worth living for."

I returned to Calcutta a year later. Bola's bed was empty. No one there even remembered him. But I did.

Since receiving her first camera and journal at ten years old, Alison Wright, a freelance photojournalist and writer, has traveled from the Arctic to the Amazon documenting the traditions and changes of endangered cultures in remote areas of the world. In 1993 she received the Dorothea Lange Award in documentary photography for her photographs of child labor in Asia. Documenting Tibetan life in exile has been her project of passion for over a decade. Her published work includes The Spirit of Tibet: Portrait of a Culture in Exile *and* A Simple Monk: Writings on the Dalai Lama, *as well as inclusion in* Wild Writing Women *and* Travelers' Tales Nepal. *She is currently working on a photo book of children around the world titled* Faces of Hope.

LEO W. BANKS

* * *

Searching for
the Good Spirit

The mysteries of the Southwest are legion.

THIS BLASTED WIND IS ALL I HAVE. IT FILLS MY HEAD. IT CLOUDS my mind. It threads my clothes. It blows sand into my mouth and brings on black clouds, the smell of rain, and voices that stand out even above the howling.

I hear children's voices, way off, in some place behind the beyond, but still clear, as though coming from lips pressed to my ear.

My partner, Edward McCain, walked off looking for the only thing photographers seek. Light. How strange to look at the world the way he does. To hunt light. To be consumed by it. To be in conversation one moment, and the light shifts, and something turns over in his brain, and he's off, chasing one ethereal, always moving, always changing commodity. Light.

My own master is no less bizarre. A spirit.

I'm approaching a canyon on the western end of the Navajo reservation. This land, particularly Begashibito Canyon, is said to be inhabited by a benevolent force called the Good Spirit.

It's a preposterous legend. Not a tale that could be told in my world without a nudge and a wink. Long beyond understanding.

But not up here, where the wind makes the rocks bow, a world of rust mesas, shimmering horizons that only get farther away as you move toward them, and moonlike ground so parched it could make a lizard weep.

I've been chasing the Good Spirit for almost two years. Several times I've come to this other world, searching. Now I feel as if I'm closing in. The children's voices pull me forward.

We're on foot, McCain and I. We had turned left off U.S. Route 160 some thirty-eight miles outside Tuba City, onto State Route 98 over Shonto Wash, then onto dusty reservation roads. We drove about thirty-five miles from the boarded-up Cow Springs Trading Post on U.S. 160 before we started walking.

They call it a canyon, but it's so shallow it hardly seems to merit the description. The English name for this place is Cow Springs Canyon. Begashibito, pronounce ba-GOSH-ibito in Navajo, means "place where the cows water."

The voices lead me down a split in the side of the wash that cuts the canyon, and I bounce on my rear end to the bottom. The wash banks are high, maybe twenty-five feet. They channel the voices and carry them to me, clear as the noon sun.

Still, I'm not sure they're real. It might just be the wind talking.

McCain heads in the opposite direction, hauling his gear over fine sand, like he's running in a dream. That's what photographers do, run in their dreams hoping to catch fleeting light.

I go a long way. I don't know how far, a mile, maybe, when a blast of thunder shakes the ground, and it occurs to me, for the first time, that I'm in danger.

I'm walking in a wash as though on a Sunday stroll, and there's a storm building. Flash flood. The single most obvious peril of the desert didn't occur to me until this instant, and even now that it has penetrated my consciousness, I feel no fear.

I keep walking toward the voices and out loud I say to myself something I don't believe: "It's the Good Spirit."

My research brought me to one brick wall after another. Talking to a Navajo about spirits is a bit like being at the boss's dinner party and mentioning the corpse propped at the head of the table.

Let me tell a story.

I'd stopped at the Old Red Lake Trading Post in Tonalea. A typical afternoon on the Big Rez. Pickup trucks whirled in, one after another, with bumper stickers that proclaimed: Rodeo!

Young men stepped out, shook off the dust, and strutted past, in uniform: slant-heel cowboy boots, turquoise rings, black Stetsons with rope hatbands and feathers dangling from the back brim. And that odd way Navajo men have of saying hello by pursing their lips. Those are the gregarious ones.

After an hour of leaning against the wall and watching the show, I went inside. The clerk was a young fellow, and beside him, at the movie-rental counter, stood three boys. They were imitating some variety of mayhem from the latest martial arts movie.

I wanted to ask about the Good Spirit. I had my presentation planned. My cover was a gum purchase. I dropped the gum on the counter. "Say, have you ever heard of a Good Spirit that inhabits the Cow Springs area?"

I swear, you would've thought I'd lit the fuse on a stick of dynamite and held it in his face. I'd noticed the corpse at the table. I pressed on, soothingly. "I read something about the

Good Spirit of Begashibito Canyon. Gets people out of jams and such."

The clerk was so nervous, he couldn't stop laughing. His shoulders shook. I took the hint and got out of there.

The truth is, stories are told of the Good Spirit. At least they're told in print. A half-century-old magazine tells of a man riding through a sandstorm along what he thought was a trail into Begashibito Canyon.

But he got lost, and the storm grew violent. He felt his horse shake in fear beneath him. Squinting, he caught sight of something moving through the swirling air ahead of him. He had no idea what it was. Desperate, with no choice but to ride or die, he urged his horse forward.

The horse, suddenly finding its legs, followed whatever it was to safety. It was the Good Spirit, the man claimed later.

Three Navajo boys wandered from their mother's sheep camp and got lost. Night fell. A search party was organized. When dawn broke, the children were seen walking serenely toward the camp. Asked how they found their way home, the oldest boy looked surprised. "Why, the man in the long coat came to us when the big star arose. We followed him."

An old woman, also on horseback, was in the canyon when a rainstorm blew in, and with it came a tremendous roar. Soaking wet, she listened to identify the sound.

Just then she saw the figure of a man walking out of the bed of the canyon wash. His head was bare, and he wore a gray robe tied with a rope at his waist and grass sandals.

"I'd no sooner cleared the wash," the old woman said, "when a great wall of water swept past, overflowing to the depth of several feet the place I had just left. I would have been slain by the Water Monster."

*

The clouds hang low now, black beasts hovering above me. The wind blows relentlessly, almost painful as it hammers away.

As I struggle against it, I'm thinking about those published legends. Preposterous, inexplicable. But I realize again, as I always do on this great and unknowable reservation, that this isn't a land of answers, only questions.

When McCain and I were wheeling along State 98, we drove over a pair of work gloves. Nothing around them, no other traffic, just two gloves.

They were on fire. Smoke rose off them, fanned by the wind. Neither of us said a word as we passed over them. A few hundred feet down the road, I couldn't stand it any longer.

"Did you see that back there?" I asked.

"I sure did."

"What the heck was it?"

"Gloves? I don't know."

McCain turned around to get a look, but by then I was swinging into a U-turn. They were exactly what they appeared to be, burning black work gloves. Only by the time we got there, one of the gloves was gone. The other was still burning.

Preposterous. Inexplicable. Like the white saddled horse we saw tied to a range fence with no rider in sight. And no place for a rider on flat landscape without buildings or concealment to the farthest limits of our vision.

Here we were chasing a spirit, and we came upon burning gloves and a riderless horse. We did what people from our world do. We joked about it, had ourselves a good laugh.

The wash zigzags across the Earth, its walls revealing deep gashes from previous floods. The sand on the wash bottom shows red, and that makes the pile of animal bones stand out. They're bleached white, scattered at my feet.

I step over them. Lightning splits the sky. It seems to bring the voices closer than ever. McCain catches up, and we crawl out of the wash and climb a hill and lie on our bellies to have a look.

Until this instant, peering over flat red tundra, I wasn't sure the voices were real. Now I see them, three children, looking tiny in the distance playing and giggling in the wash. Nearby stretches a cornfield, with two women working it.

The scene appears idyllic. Like a painting. Peaceful to watch.

McCain and I kick around the idea of approaching and asking about the Good Spirit. But that would be foolhardy, two strangers appearing out of a wash to inquire about an apparition.

Reluctantly, feeling we again have failed to find what we were looking for, we drive on steep dirt hills out of Begashibito Canyon to Shonto Plateau and Indian 16. The long-expected downpour starts the moment we reach pavement.

"Wow," I say to the racket of the rain beating on the car.

"Yeah," says McCain, "if we hadn't gotten out of there when we did…"

He looks over at me, and his voice trails off. Nothing more is said. But I can see the realization in his eyes. I recognize it because I have the same thought:

Those children in the wash were protected, and they knew it. So were we, only the dictates of our world concealed it from us until just now. In following their gleeful voices, maybe we found the Good Spirit, too.

We stop joking about the burning gloves and the riderless horse and the rest of it. We don't understand what any of it means, if there is anything to understand.

But we no longer laugh. We drive on quietly in the rain.

Leo W. Banks has been writing about the Southwest for various newspapers and magazines for twenty-five years. He also has written several books of Western history. For a brief time two decades ago, he taught school on the Navajo reservation in Shiprock, New Mexico. He lives in Tucson, Arizona.

★ ★ ★

Ego Te Absolvo

*In Argentina, mimicry proves
to be the best defense.*

*Ego te absolvo a peccatis tuis in nomine Patris et Filii
et Spiritus Sancti. Amen.*

I absolve you of your sins in the name of the Father and of
the Son and of the Holy Ghost. Amen.

As it is in many Latin American countries, it is a custom
among observant Catholics here to cross themselves whenever they pass a church of their faith. However they are traveling—walking, bus, train, car—they cross themselves as they
rumble past. Just the act of watching people do that makes me
feel protected, as it must do even more so for those who make
the sign.

It's a fleeting, discreet movement, which though it takes
place in a public setting, is not at all a public moment. Up,
down, left, right, kiss the back of the thumb.

...in nomine Patris et Filii et Spiritus Sancti.

I'm not Catholic and don't need to be, I think, to feel that
my fellow passengers make the sign of the cross for as many
reasons as there are people doing it. Maybe deeply held con-

viction or a parochial school autonomic reflex, or a momentary reconnect with eternity in a life that is otherwise temporal, secular, and self-absorbed—nobody knows. In the darkened back seats of the Avenida Maipú bus at 1:00 A.M., it's one of the rare human acts utterly without political motivation. A handshake with the unseen God and the faith that He is there to reciprocate.

I spend between two and three hours a day on mass transit to and from the office. It's a complicated trip from the backwaters of the suburbs of Buenos Aires, hitting the whole sampler of urban public conveyance: bus, train, subway and my own two feet. Occasionally, it's the commute from hell, but it gives me a lot of time to read and watch faces so I mostly forgive it. *Te absolvo.*

Among the faces is a dark-haired woman on the subway, early thirties, office worker by her clothes, but not management. A book has her full attention. Her head tilts forward to reveal an area of thinning hair on top near the back that is evolving into a strikingly noticeable bald spot on an otherwise attractive head, face, and body. Men expect to lose their hair. How terrible it must be for a woman.

A man who shares my subway car almost daily (inbound, third car from the end so as to be right by the exit when it stops), has a red birthmark around his eye. It is his further misfortune that the blemish is not dark enough to be an obvious birthmark, which people would notice and then studiously ignore and make no comment about. It's just red enough to resemble the result of a run-in with a door three days ago. I know it's permanent because I've seen it for months, but strangers who sit next to him say, "Ooo, I see the missus clobbered you a good one." He gets this a lot, and whatever he thinks, it's probably way past: What did I ever do to deserve this?

When I round the corner of the stairs heading for the lower level of Retiro Station every morning at 7:21 there are one or two or three young boys asleep on the bare floor next to the wall in this unheated passageway. Sheltered from the wind, but not the cold, the boys have their sweatshirts and dirty jackets pulled as far over their heads as they can get them. What is most jarring is that these are young children, eight, maybe twelve years old and they *live* at Retiro Station. They are still asleep at that hour, and commuters hurrying past set food down beside them. But it's all snack cakes and cookies—coffee break bullshit food at the Twinkies end of the nutrition spectrum.

No matter how many times you see them, it's not something a person can get used to. And this is nothing. I've seen thousands more doorway children ("gamines") in Colombia and Mexico. There must be zillions in Brazil, where cast-off children live downtown, begging and stealing or selling their bodies. A mini-scandal erupted in Rio de Janeiro a couple of years ago when it was revealed that a businessman's organization had hired thugs to go through the alleys at night and kill the street children to thin their numbers.

When blessing-counting time rolls around, as it does for all of us now and then, a millisecond on the street in the presence of poverty, is all most of us need to dredge up a sincere "there but for the grace of God." It's so easy to find a reason to make the sign of the cross.

Misereatur tui omnipotens Deus, et dimissis peccatis tuis, perducat te ad vitam aeternam.

May Almighty God have mercy on you, forgive you your sins, and bring you to everlasting life.

My observation is that one or two per bus or train car, and every fourth or fifth taxi driver, will do the sign of the cross. When I first came to Buenos Aires I noticed it, but it took a few weeks for me to associate it with passing a church. There is one spot on my train commute, near the horse track, where I still haven't been able to locate the church. People swirl their hands across their foreheads and chests as we zip past what looks to me like a small string of establishments that includes a fitness center and a bar. Maybe one used to be there.

I'm sitting on a crowded late night bus from the train station, the final leg of my homeward commute. I never met a Third World country (or "emerging nation" as we like to call ourselves) where the buses aren't packed solid all the time. It's easy to see why. Most can't afford a car. It's related to why you see so many young people passionately kissing on the park benches, in the grass, leaning against lamp posts on the corner. No car, you live with your parents; the park is the most intimate setting you've got. It's here or cold turkey abstinence. We're talking extreme heavy passion under the statue of the liberator, José de San Martín. It can be quite an aesthetic experience for the passerby.

The bus is coming up on a small cathedral and I'm playing a game I invented where I try to predict who of those around me will make the sacred gesture. I'm nearly always wrong. I think I've guessed right maybe once, and that was a nun so it really doesn't count. It isn't always the little old lady or the man put on the social margins by his physical deformity. Often it's the hunky, young Turk fast-tracking at the firm and the slinky secretary who pay homage to the custom. I have yet to see the sign of the cross made by a couple, a man and woman together, for whatever reason.

Standing in front of me on the last bus of the night is a red-haired man in his twenties. Lean and strong, he hasn't shaved in four, maybe five days. On his arm is a tattoo of what looks like an oak tree with a big grinning skull imbedded in the trunk. A snake crawls out one of the eye sockets. As we pass under a street lamp, light skims across the man's bare arm. It's not an oak tree; it's a naked woman. Boy am I tired.

He scowls through eyes dark and twisted. He looks over at me in my hoity-toity suit and wimp-ass tie, registering angry confusion. He keeps looking at me and I stare back at him way too long. I'm fascinated and I realize I'm not breaking eye contact as the rules call for. What do I think I'm doing? Larry, are you nuts? You have five children to think of. I look away, but he doesn't, not for a long time. I'm dead meat.

I would like to say that in the moment of our contact I could sense in his dark recesses, a tiny spark of original humanity, something in there a compassionate man could reach out to and connect with, given enough time.. A beautiful thought, and it would be so very Bing Crosby wouldn't it? Like in the classic *Going My Way*—jaunty Father O'Malley in black clericals and a straw boater turns a hardened street gang into St. Dominic's choir. Maybe God was speaking to my heart at that moment. I'm now looking for the humanity in my knuckle-dragging brother, and for the Bing Crosby in me, but it's a tough sell either way. What would Father O'Malley say to him? Hi there, I guess your mother's a troglodyte?

The problem is, there doesn't seem to be anybody human at home. Not even remotely so. To the very core of his bottom corpuscle, he looks like Central Casting's alienated postal worker, Arlo Guthrie's "biggest, meanest, mother-raper of them all."

Then it hits me. I am so totally wrong about people that this guy will probably defy all odds and cross himself when we pass the church. He's probably a future saint, on his way to donate a kidney. What he'll probably do is cross himself. And then after that, he'll come over and kill me for looking at him too long because…well, because this is Argentina.

I'm nearly ready to bet the ranch on it. We pass the church. He doesn't.

But I do.

I have to say there is something foundationally powerful in the Catholic tradition. Something there for me. I admire their…I don't know exactly what…the faith they place in faith?

I remember an old woman in Oaxaca, Mexico in 1973, advancing the last hundred meters to the basilica doors on her bare knees. She inched forward a foot or two at a time along a path of sharp stones that cut her legs. She wrung her hands and cried and cried and cried, wailing loudly, fervently. Whatever had broken her heart, the stones had nothing to do with it.

Two small daughters or granddaughters placed a scarf on the ground for her to crawl over. As she passed, they retrieved it and brought it around in front for her to pass over again. The scarf and the hem of her dress quickly became streaked with blood.

She made the sign of the cross.

Dominus noster Jesus Christus te absolvat…

Our Lord Jesus Christ absolve you…

I was a hitchhiker just out of communication grad school, a *mochilero* with a backpack and jeans. I felt self-conscious and embarrassed but I stopped and watched her anyway. Other people were walking past like this happens every day. I think I may have promised myself that as payment for my intrusion, I would remember what I was seeing. Someday I would tell somebody about this and maybe it would help them.

As it turns out, I am the one helped. My beliefs and life and the teachings of the past twenty-four years liberate me to be as fully one with anyone's earnest attempt to touch God, in any faith, as my own maturity will allow. My God tells me that

before it's over, everyone of us will be that old woman at least
one time. If I want it to be my course, and risk the risk, and
set my heart ablaze daily, and toil in the vineyards of the Lord
and be about my Father's business, then I can be her lighted
candle. I am free to be all faiths, to make all Gods my God,
all people my people. I am unificationist. I make the sign of
the cross.

*In the process of organizing international conferences and media fact-
finding trips, Larry R. Moffitt has visited more than seventy countries
in the past two decades. From the Amazon River to North Korea,
from Angola and the Mayan jungles of Guatemala to Soviet and
post-Soviet Russia, he has mispronounced his way around the world
and eaten the unidentifiable. His checkered past has included work as
a farmer and beekeeper, short story writer, newsletter editor, stand-up
comedian, and bad poet. He is currently a vice president of United
Press International. He now lives in Washington, D.C.*

MARIANNE DRESSER

✶ ✶ ✶

Passing Through

You are more than you think.

IT'S ONLY A SHORT WALK THROUGH THE SMALL VILLAGE OF
Bodh Gaya, a quarter-mile or so down the main dirt road to
the *vihar*, the Burmese monastery and pilgrims' lodge at the
edge of town where I am staying. But to reach the road I have
to pass the gauntlet of beggars lining the Mahabodhi's outer
wall. They arrange themselves in an intricate hierarchy: first,
the wild-eyed sadhus, renunciants lost in an ecstasy of self-
chosen self-abnegation, clothed in little more than the sacred
dirt of Mother India. Next to them, the more conventional
beggars whose abject poverty and homelessness, not sanc-
tioned by religious choice, is correspondingly less auspicious.

Last in line, well after devotees' purses have already been
opened and closed again, are those whose credentials are simply their tortured and incomplete bodies, entire limbs missing
or ending in puzzling shapes. With cruel logic, the begging
business deems that contributions to the holy poor carry a
greater karmic reward than giving to those who are merely
destitute for all the usual reasons—caste and color, bad luck or

bad timing on the cosmic Wheel of Fortune. I dispense a few rupees at strategic intervals, hoping the greatest number receive part of a contribution that will never be enough. A dull ache accompanies this brief ritual; I have grown accustomed to its presence in my sternum.

Once past the patient gallery of beggars, I'm immediately assailed by the bright cries and alert glances of the rickshaw-*wallahs* who gather just outside the temple grounds. Eager to win my paltry patronage for a five-minute ride, they shout, "Sister!" "Look, sister!" "Best ride here, sister!" By now, after three months of this nightly ritual, we mostly recognize one another. Though I'm not a likely customer they give me their most eloquent entreaties anyway, eyes smiling. I smile back, nod gently, do not break my stride. I stroll out into the main road, past the closed-up box-carts that by day are one-man shops dispensing necessities: candles, date-expired antibiotics, warm, syrupy soft drinks. I can feel the pores of my sandaled feet soaking up warm dust. Woodsmoke, spices sizzling in oil, sweet sandalwood, dung—a rich brew of smells crowds for space in the air, clouding my nostrils and stinging my eyes.

Down the road, past the souvenir hawkers, who all offer the same cheaply printed postcards, the same rough-hewn replicas of the sublime stone deities scattered throughout the temple. In my first few weeks in Bodh Gaya, I had spent many an evening perusing these offerings, choosing the little figure whose creator, with the luckiest slip of the chisel, had rendered the archaic smile intact. But I no longer thirsted for the perfect bodhisattva. The makeshift altar in my quiet, small room at the *vihar* already had a full complement of tiny images. And behind them rested a leaf from the sacred Bo tree that floated to the ground as I sat beneath its protective canopy. Dried by the Indian heat, the tear-shaped pipal leaf had become a crisp, slightly shrunken but perfect replica of itself.

On the other side of the road, groups of travelers and pilgrims congregate at the *chai* shops, dipping *gulab jamen* into cups of the strong milky brew and talking animatedly. The foreigners indulge in the queasy pleasure of comparing digestive-tract horror stories, another ritual I used to take part in. Lately, the brief exchanges, nods, and smiles I exchange with the familiar locals along the road are all the society I crave. I walk past the whitewashed statue of Gandhi, his slightly comical oversize eyeglasses rendered in thick black enamel. In Bodh Gaya, the architect of India's liberation is just one more saint, a latecomer to the vast Hindu pantheon that keeps growing like a benign B-movie monster. A reflex of the spiritual generosity that recognizes and accepts all exemplars of holiness—from the Buddha to Christ.

I walk past the snack vendor who always charges me an extra rupee or two for a packet of stale popcorn. He has liquid brown eyes and such a beatific smile that I pay the difference willingly. I pass the shop of the Muslim tailor, working under a single bare bulb suspended by a thin wire over his elderly machine. I know the shoemaker's shop by the brightly colored poster of Ambedkar, the modern-day founder of a religion for his kind, India's untouchables. I nod to the cloth merchant who sold me the *khadi* cloth for the loose, long shirts I wear, comfortable in the close heat and safely androgynous. He is lounging with his cronies on a thick woven rug, framed by colorful bolts of fabric. He sips his tea, laughs and gestures, looking all the world like a thirteenth-century pasha.

Quieter now, farther away from the temples and monasteries and the religious heart of town. Bodh Gaya is home to a host of major and minor deities, and a yearly round of festivals in their honor—raucous crowds celebrating the Goddess Durga; the whole town lit by thousands of flickering candles for Diwali, the Festival of Lights; the Mahabodhi ablaze with oil-lamp offerings to the Buddha; Surya Puja, when the village women bathe in the river at dawn and pass out *prasad*, divinely blessed food, like candy at Halloween. At *puja* time, the town is a booming spiritual marketplace serving the steady stream of wayfarers who buy the small terra-cotta figures for worship, the candles and incense to burn, the flowers to scatter. The streets are clogged with ecstasy, and all those transient prayerful bodies need food to eat and a place to sleep. Now, between festivals, it's just a few itinerant pilgrims and me, on this dirt road dodging bicycle rickshaws and sacred cows.

Buzzing clouds of insects clot the meagerly interspersed streetlights. A soft, luminous shudder, thousands of tiny shadows. I walk steadily through the circles of light, passing quickly through the fluttering wave of small frantic life-forms brushing against the bare skin of my arms and neck. I know to keep my mouth closed and breathe out slowly. Off to the right is the river Falgu, its turgid, broad, brown sweep dissected by a sliver of reflected moonlight. Flat cow-shaped silhouettes stand in matte-black relief on the near shore. The failing light mercifully obscures the river's slow cargo of animal carcasses, debris, and the occasional half-burned body, its soul long since released into the ocean of time from the charnel grounds upstream.

On the road, I'm nearly home now. Russet twilight stains the western sky long after the sun has slipped behind the fringe of trees at the edge of the world. The beauty of it commands my attention, the tenacity leaves me breathless. A subtle pressure in the air: the body of time. Countless births and deaths and rebirths, and in between the elastic span that we call life. This place is very old, and weary, and yet an invincible spirit permeates everything, animates even the tiny diamonds of light darting off the water.

I take refuge in these images: the molten river, a gnarled tree, a brackish pool in which a single white lotus, now closing gently against the evening coolness, will again miraculously bloom. Three women pass me, giggling at my cropped hair, my indeterminate features. Do they think I'm a boy? Do they know I'm a woman and wonder at my aloneness, here on this road? Each one wears the vermilion streak lining the part in her glossy black hair—the furrow split by the plow—signifying her married status. A young tea vendor pours a cup of milky brew the color of his palms and flashes a radiant gap-toothed grin at me. "*Chai*, sister?" he beckons earnestly, forcing another refusal from me; the momentum of my stride carries me on. A thin old man drives his dusty gray and blue-black bullocks leisurely toward the patchy fields on the riverbank. Their massive haunches heave a lazy rhythm as they move past me, their tails halfheartedly flicking away flies. I run my hand over their broad backs, touch the pungent skin of the world.

Where am I in all this? A spectator, a ghost?

A guest.

Suddenly I become lighter, transparent. Things pass through. My senses are as permeable as a membrane. Someone is laughing.

Walking on a dusty road in the gauzy half-light of an evening passing into night, lost to the gracious anonymity afforded by the gathering darkness. For an instant that stretches to infinity, there is no "I," only seeing. A moment of freedom from the bounded entity, the name and story that shores up the fragile and tenuous sense of self on which a life—my life—has been built in great earnestness.

The earliest texts speak of the moment of the Buddha's realization as "burning down the house." The figure on the road is straw, dry kindling, just waiting for a spark.

Marianne Dresser's travel stories have appeared in Food: A Taste of the Road, The Road Within, Lesbian Travels: A Literary Companion, Turning Wheel: Journal of Engaged Buddhism, *and* Passionfruit. *She is the editor of* Buddhist Women on the Edge: Contemporary Perspectives from the Western Frontier *and serves as Editor for the Numata Center for Buddhist Translation and Research. She lives in Oakland, California, with her canine companion, Bodhi, and wanders off to Asia as often as she can, most recently returning to India to attend teachings given by His Holiness the Dalai Lama.*

PART TWO

HEALING

TIM O'REILLY

* * *

Walking the Kerry Way

*A candle in a dark church
illumines family history.*

I HADN'T SPENT MUCH TIME WITH MY BROTHER FRANK SINCE he was about twelve years old, back in 1973. That was the year I'd gotten engaged to a non-Catholic, and my parents wouldn't let me bring her home because "it would scandalize the children." I was nineteen and equally sure of myself, so I refused to come home without her.

I finally gave in seven years later, when my father's health was failing, and went home for a visit alone. After that, my parents also relented, and met my wife and three-year-old daughter for the first time. Our mutual stubbornness had cost us precious time together as a family, a loss made especially poignant by my father's death six months later.

My relationship with my younger brother and sisters took years to recover. By the time I came home after my long exile, Frank was away at college, and thereafter we'd met mainly at family holidays and reunions. Still, we'd found many common interests and a mutual admiration. Both of us were entrepreneurs—I in publishing, he in construction—and both of us had struggled with how to build a business with a heart, a business that served its employees as well as its customers. In many ways, our lives were mirror images, seven years apart.

But there was one big crack in the mirror, one gulf between us that we skirted politely (most of the time): while I had long ago left the church, Frank remained a committed Catholic. He had also retained an abiding love for Ireland, to which he had returned again and again with my father, mother, and sisters in the years when I was persona non grata. He and my father had gone for many a tramp around Killarney, the town where my father was born, and where my aunt still lives. Mangerton, Torc, and the McGillicuddy Reeks were more than names to Frank; hikes on the slopes of these mountains were the source of the richest memories of his childhood and young adulthood.

I envied Frank the time he'd spent in Ireland with my father, and I'd always wanted to spend more time there myself. When my mother suggested that Frank and I might want to walk part of the Kerry Way together (a higher altitude walking version of the Ring of Kerry), we both jumped at the chance. I had a week between a talk I was due to give in Rome and another in London. It was March—not the best time to visit Ireland—but Frank could get free, and with his eighth child on the way, it was now or never.

We set out from Killarney on a blustery day. Though neither of us had done much recent hiking, we had an ambitious itinerary, about eighteen miles a day for the next five days. We were planning on staying each night at bed & breakfasts along the way, but we still carried packs with plenty of extra clothes.

The first day took us through Killarney National Park, up around the back of Torc, then down across the road to Moll's Gap and into the Black Valley. The hike took more out of us than we expected, and we tottered the last few miles, grateful that our guest house was at the near end of "town" (a sprinkling of houses spread over the better part of a mile).

After a hearty dinner of local lamb chops, though, things began to look up, so when Frank confessed that it was his wife's birthday, and that he wanted to go a mile up the road to the valley's only public phone, outside the youth hostel and the church, to call her, I agreed to go along. It was pitch dark by then, and raining to boot. We managed to stick to the road, though, and eventually came to the phone. Unfortunately, Angelique was not at home. How about going in to say a rosary for her, he asked?

Now, I hadn't said the rosary for over twenty years, and wasn't sure I even remembered how the "Hail Mary" went, but I agreed.

The church was open, of course, its outer door swinging in the wind. In Ireland, at least in the back country, the church is never closed. There was no electricity, and only a single candle burning by the altar. The wind howled outside, the door banged open and shut. We began to pray.

Frank helped me recall the words; the memories I'd never lost. When we were small, the rosary, even more than dinner (where my mother never sat down till everyone else had eaten), was the time the family was all together. As we droned aloud through the decades, the joyful, the glorious, and the sorrowful mysteries, I remembered my father's passing.

He had had a heart attack. He knew himself to be a dead man, he said. He was met by Mary, Saint Joseph, and surprisingly, the devil. He begged for more time to make his peace with his family, and his wish was granted. The doctors brought him back, and as he lay in the hospital, intubated and unable to speak, he was desperate to communicate with each of us, scrawling on a small white slate. He wanted to reply to my letter, he said.

I had written him a few weeks before, telling him that even though I had left the church, I had absorbed so much of him, his belief, his moral values, his desire to be good, and to do good. I didn't want him to think he had failed. His short, so poignant reply, written on a slate and soon erased, but burned forever in my memory: "God forgive me, a sinner." His apology for the long years we had not spent together: "I only wanted you to be with us in paradise." The desire for togetherness in a world to come had become a wedge between us.

As he recovered over the next few days, he was a different man. He had always embodied for me so much of the stern, dogmatic side of Catholicism. Now, in the face of death, all that was stripped away, and the inner core of spirituality was revealed. His passion for his God was the heart of his life. How could I have never seen it before? So many of us build a shell around who we really are; our inner world is as untouchable as the heart of an oyster, till forces greater than we are pry us apart. Now, all was exposed. "I never showed you the face of Christ when you were small," he told my brother James. Well, he showed it to us then. It's as if he'd been turned inside out, and all the love and spiritual longing that had been hidden by his shyness and his formality were shining out like the sun.

Three weeks later, the time he had asked for was up. He had another attack, and this time he went for good.

We had taken him back to Ireland to bury him. It was a magical day, early April but beautiful as only a spring day in Ireland can be beautiful, a day of radiance stolen from the gloom. The funeral mass in the cathedral was concelebrated by thirty or forty priests: his two brothers, his childhood friends, and many others come to honor the life of one of Killarney's dear sons now coming home for good. (He had himself studied for the priesthood before deciding to pursue family life instead; his brothers Frank and Seumas had become senior in two of Ireland's great orders of priests, the Franciscans and the Columbans.)

He was buried in a Franciscan robe. He had long been a member of "the little order of Saint Francis," a lay organization devoted to Franciscan ideals. We learned then of small penances he would do, like tying rough twine around his waist under his clothes. As if it were still the Middle Ages! I would have scoffed, but I'd seen the light shining through him when impending death had pried all his coverings away.

Afterwards, the four sons, Sean, James, Frank, and I, walked behind the hearse up the main street of the town. As the funeral procession passed, those walking in the opposite direction turned and took "the three steps of mercy," walking with the procession. The depths of Ireland's Catholic legacy was never so clear as when a group of loutish youths, who might have been a street gang anywhere else, bowed their heads and turned to take the three steps with us.

As we turned up the road to Aghadoe cemetery, a breeze blew, and the blossoms fell from the trees onto the coffin. If it had been a movie, I would have laughed. It's never that perfect! Except it was.

The cemetery, crowned with the ruins of a sixth century chapel, looks down on the lakes of Killarney. Ham-handed farmers (my father's schoolmates) helped us carry the coffin over rough ground to the family plot. Normally, after the service, we would have all left, and "the lads" would have filled in the grave. But we wanted a last farewell, so we sent the lads on their way, and Sean, James, Frank, and I filled in the grave.

Now, eighteen years later, I was back in Ireland. My tiredness fell away. I was at the heart of my father's mystery, the place where he had turned his passionate heart to God, and the place where he had wrapped it round with rituals that had kept me from seeing its purity and its strength.

Somehow, Frank had seen through the ritual, had shared in it and sunk his roots to the same deep place. I was honored that he was opening the door for me as well. "Hail Mary, full of grace, the Lord is with thee..."

There are a thousand ways to God. Let us all honor the ways that others have found.

The next few days we wore our legs off, as the paths became wilder. The worst of it was the aptly named Lack Road, which our guidebook insisted had been used to drive cattle to market "within living memory." We couldn't see how you could drive a mountain goat herd across it now, as we picked our way down an impossibly steep slope. We understood why our aunt, who had worked in Kerry Mountain Rescue, had insisted we pack so many extra clothes. Turn an ankle out here, and you're many hours from help, with changeable weather bringing freezing rain at any moment. At one point, the trail, which had us up to our knees in mud at many a point, vanished beneath ten feet of water, only to reappear tantalizingly on the other side, with no apparent way across. Ireland is a wilder country than many people realize.

On the fourth day, we came round the crest of a hill and saw the ocean spread out below us. Thirty or forty miles back the other way, we could see the gleaming lakes of Killarney, and amazingly enough, the green below Aghadoe. We could see many of the passes we'd picked our way through over the last few days, the miles that had lent soreness to our feet.

Along the way, we had talked through much of the old pain of the lost years, we'd shared dreams of the present and the future, but as we went on, we'd mostly fallen into a friendly silence. The old magic of Ireland was driving our reflections inward, recreating in us the unique Irish temper—passion and wildness and boggy depths alternating with conviviality, and ending up in quietness—a mirror of the landscape and the changing weather.

Tim O'Reilly is the founder and CEO of O'Reilly & Associates, a technical information company involved in publishing, conferences, and open source software. He is a co-founder of Travelers' Tales and is a contributing editor when his brothers hold his feet to the fire.

KENT E. ST. JOHN

✦ ✦ ✦

The Devil's Wind

Even a bitter harvest must end.

As I stepped out of the wine cellar and into the wind, a strong feeling of being pulled came over me: I was drawn up toward the cathedral by an unknown source. The empty streets were soon filled with a soul-clutching sound, the vibrations swirling around in the increasing wind. The vibrations soon turned into mournful but melodic words. The only lights visible this cold, late February night were focused on the single-spired beauty of Strasbourg's Gothic cathedral and nothing else. The only sound was the lone voice, incomprehensible yet full of meaning. A solitary figure in the cathedral square slowly revealed itself, clad in dark cloak and fur-topped hat, and I realized the source of the unearthly sound. After I listened in rapture for what seemed hours, the figure beckoned me closer. As I approached, the large bearded man smiled and offered me some of his meager refreshments, bread and water. The voice belonged to him, to Emmanuel Michalski, and the words were Hebrew. It seems Emmanuel sings here at the cathedral to remind people of Sturthof/Natzweiler, the only Nazi concentration camp that was situated on French soil, and the 44,623 souls that passed through there.

"Why on such a cold windy night?" I asked.

"Because of the devil, the cathedral, and the wind," he replied.

Seeing my incomprehension, Emmanuel told me of the legend. It is said that when the devil heard about the splendors of the new cathedral he decided to see for himself. The devil summoned the wind and rode on its back into Strasbourg. When he arrived and saw the magnificent building dedicated to God and light, and not to the powers of his darkness, the devil erupted with a great rage. As the devil rode the wind around and around the monumental edifice, his anger grew until he stormed off. He was so incensed, he left the great wind behind, hoping that it would become a disruptive force for those entering God's house of worship.

Three centuries later, even on a summer's day, a cold brisk wind can be felt circling just around the cathedral. As pilgrims and tourists alike pull up their collars and wraps and enter one of France's most beautiful cathedrals, it is evident that the devil's wind has not deterred the human appreciation of works dedicated to light. Emmanuel Michalski has taken a different approach; he uses the devil's wind as a vehicle to spread words of hope, remembrance, and faith.

And so I decided to go to Sturthof/Natzweiler on my next trip to Alsace. A cold wet wind blew off the Vosges Mountains down into the valley, and my stomach was clenched in a tight ball. When I arrived at the camp, my eyes strayed up to the mountains looking for something more serene, much like the prisoners may have. Ghostly patches of fog streamed passed the barbed wire fence as I entered. Even knowing I could leave, a chill jolted my spine. This was to be my first visit into a world only glimpsed in movies and old newsreels. With all tours in French, I was given support material in English. Sturthof's beginning followed the pattern that the camp of Mathausen in Austria did.

In 1940 prisoners built the camp in atrocious conditions, the objective being to kill off most during the work. Those who entered were given categories:

- red for politicians
- purple for religious believers
- black for Gypsies and nonconformists
- pink for homosexuals
- green for common criminals
- yellow stars for the Jewish

The thought that family, friends, and loved ones fit every color and category caused a deep wrenching in my gut. Worse yet was the terrible thought that some would have been made human guinea pigs for the medical experiments by Sturthof's doctors-come-torturers. As I entered the National Necropolis with its 1,120 graves, the mist in my eyes blurred the names…the family, friends, and loved ones touched by Nazi cruelty. Wandering around the compound I came upon a sign that read, *"Lanterre Des Morts."* As I pulled out my French-English dictionary, a clutch at my elbow froze me. A small elderly gentleman asked *"Americain?"* *"Oui, je suis Americain,"* I answered. "I am Mr. Muller and I will tell you what the sign says," he said.

Mr. Muller said the sign pointed out the field where the ashes of the cremated prisoners were spread. Suddenly a huge sob broke the silence between us and Mr. Muller's shoulders shook. I clasped the old gentlemen tightly, trying to comfort what I assumed to be the haunted memory of family and friends who had passed through the camp. I led his frail body to a wooden bench as I felt all his control seep away.

After about an hour, Mr. Muller mumbled some words. I tried to comfort him by telling him those he lost at the camp would be honored by his visit. Suddenly his head dropped to his chest and another cry came from deep within his body. "I was a guard here," he gasped. At first a wave of nausea came over me like a cold wind. I pulled back as if I had been struck by lightning. Then I sensed that I may have been one of the only people that this man had ever told that fact to. "What brought you back, Mr. Muller?" I asked.

Mr. Muller, with red-rimmed eyes, told me about a cold February night when on a visit to Strasbourg he heard a mournful yet melodic voice that drew him to the cathedral. That voice belonged to Emmanuel Michalski, the very same voice that drew me in on a cold February night. It appears Emmanuel is indeed putting the "Devil's Wind" to good use, calling for a pilgrimage to look deep within.

Kent E. St. John is a contributing editor for Transitions Abroad *magazine and* GoNomad.com *as well as a staff writer and public relations manager for* Places *magazine. He is currently at work on his first book,* Be Our Guest, *tales of press trips. He now listens to the wind.*

PHIL COUSINEAU

⋆ ⋆ ⋆

The Longing

*Two brothers explore the center
of the universe.*

TOGETHER WITH MY BROTHER PAUL, I TOOK THE LONG BOAT
ride up the Mekong River in Cambodia to see one of the
great riddles of the ancient world, the sacred sprawl of ruined
temples and palaces that a twelfth-century traveler said
"housed numerous marvels."

On our first morning at the walled city of Angkor Wat, we
witnessed a glorious sunrise over its lotus-crowned towers,
then began the ritual walk up the long bridgeway toward the
sanctuary. Our arms were draped across each other's shoulders.
Our heads shook at the impossibly beautiful sight of the "marvelous enigma" that early European chroniclers regarded as
one of the Wonders of the World, and later colonialists described as rivaling the divinely inspired architecture of
Solomon.

We walked as if in a fever-dream. Halfway down the cause-
way, we paused to take in the beauty of the shifting light. We
snapped a few photographs of the *nagas*, the five-headed stone
serpents that undulated along the moat, and of the chiseled

lacework in the colossal gateway looming before us, then grinned at each other and took a deep breath of the morning air. At that moment, we noticed a gray-robed Buddhist nun limping by us on her way to the temple. Her head was shaved and bronzed. When she drew even with us, I held out an offering, which she calmly accepted with stumps where once had been hands. Stunned, I then realized why she had been walking as if on stilts. Her feet had been severed at the ankle, and she was hobbling on the knobs of her ankles. I was stricken with images of her mutilation by the demonic Khmer Rouge, then wondered if she'd been a victim of one of the 11 million landmines forgotten in the forests, fields, and roads of Cambodia.

Her eyes met mine with a gaze of almost surreal serenity. Utterly moved, we offered a few dollars for the shrine in the temple. She calmly accepted the donation in a small woven bag, bowed, and limped away, like a thin-legged crane moving stiffly through the mud of one of the nearby ponds.

The encounter with the Cambodian nun was an ominous way to begin our visit, a gift briefly disguised as a disturbance. Her enigmatic smile eerily anticipated the expression on the sculptured faces of the fifty-four giant bodhisattvas that loomed in the Holy of Holies above the nearby pyramid temples of the Bayon. Each time I met their timeless gaze, my heart leapt. As the lotus ponds and pools throughout the complex were created to reflect each work of religious art, the faces of the bodhisattvas and the nun mirrored each other. I began to think of the nun as the embodiment of the Bodhisattvas Avalokiteshvara, the god of inexhaustible compassion, who has come to symbolize the miracle of Angkor for millions of pilgrims.

How far does your forgiveness reach? the sculpted faces ask from a thousand statues.

As far as prayers allow, the nun's eyes seemed to respond.

I rambled through the ruins with my brother for the next several hours, stunned by our sheer good fortune of being there. The Angkor complex was destroyed in the fifteenth century, then forgotten for 400 years and overrun with the stone-strangling vines of the jungle. Marveling at the beauty laced with terror in the stories of our young Cambodian guide (who told us the local villagers believed that Angkor was built by angels and giants), time seemed poised on the still-point of the world. This was more than an architectural curiosity, a pious parable of fleeting glory; it was a microcosm of the universe itself. According to scholars, the walls, moats, and soaring terraces represented the different levels of existence itself. The five towers of Angkor symbolized the five peaks of Mount Meru, the center of the world in Hindu cosmology. This was the world mountain in stone, a monumental mandala encompassed by moats that evoked the oceans. A visit was an accomplishment demanding the rigorous climbing of precipitously steep staircases, built that way not without reason.

"It is clear," wrote Vice Admiral Bonard, an early colonialist, "that the worshiper penetrating the temple was intended to have a tangible sense of moving to higher and higher levels of initiation." Our three days stretched on. The hours seemed to contain days, the days held weeks, as in all dreamtime adventures. We were graced with one strangely moving encounter after another. Silently, we mingled with saffron-robed monks who had walked hundreds of miles in the footsteps of their ancestors from Cambodia, Thailand, India, and Japan to pray in the sanctuary of a place believed for a thousand years to be the center of the world. Gratefully, we traded road stories with travelers who'd been through Burma, Vietnam, and China. After dark, we read the accounts of fellow pilgrims who had been making the arduous trek here by foot for centuries, from China and Japan in ancient times, then by car from France and England, and by boat from America.

Though neither Buddhist nor Hindu, wandering through the site I was more than smitten by the romancing of old stones. In the uncanny way of spiritually magnetized centers of pilgrimage, I felt a wonderful calm exploring the derelict pavilions, abandoned libraries, and looted monasteries. My imagination was animated by the strange and wonderful challenge to fill in what time had destroyed, thrilling to the knowledge that tigers, panthers, and elephants still roamed over the flagstones of these shrines when Angkor was rediscovered in the 1860s.

But through our visit the dark thread ran.

With every step through the ghostly glory of the ancient temple grounds, it was impossible not to be reminded of the scourge of Pol Pot, the ever-present threat of historical chaos. The maimed children and fierce soldiers we encountered everywhere were grim evidence of a never-ending war. Once upon a time, foreigners were spared the horrors of remote revolutions, but no more. In a local English-language newspaper, we read that Pol Pot had ordered the executions of three Australian tourists, saying only, "Crush them."

Overshadowing even this were the twinges of guilt I felt for having undertaken the journey—Jo, my partner back in San Francisco, was seven months pregnant with our baby. Though she was selflessly supportive, I was uneasy. So why make such a risky journey?

To fulfill a vow.

Twice in the previous fifteen years, my plans to make the long trek to the ruins of Angkor had been thwarted at the Thai-Cambodia border. Dreading that war might break out again and the borders clamp shut for another twenty years, I believed that the research trip my brother and I were on in the Philippines serendipitously offered a last chance to fulfill a promise to my father.

On my eleventh birthday, he had presented me with a book, not a Zane Grey Western or the biography of my hometown baseball hero, Al Kaline, that I had asked for, but a book with a bronze-tinted cover depicting sculptures of fabulous creatures from a distant world. These creatures were not from a phantasmagorical planet out of science fiction, but the long-forgotten world of the Khmers, the ancient civilization that had built Angkor.

From that moment on, the book came to symbolize for me the hidden beauty of the world. With the transportive magic that only books possess, it offered a vision of the vast world outside of my small hometown in Michigan; it set a fire in my heart and through the years inspired in me the pilgrim's desire to see this wondrous place for myself.

When my father became ill in the fall of 1984, I drove cross-country from San Francisco to Detroit to see him and, in an effort to lift his spirits, promised him that when he recovered we would travel together. I tried to convince him that after years of unfulfilled plans to see Europe, we would travel together to Amsterdam and visit van Gogh's nephew, whom he had once guided on a personal tour through Ford's River Rouge complex in Dearborn. After Holland, I suggested, we could take the train to Périgueux in southern France and track down the story of our ancestors who had left there in 1678. Then, I said haltingly, we could take a direct flight from Paris to Phnom Penh and visit Angkor Wat. He seemed pleased by the former, puzzled by the latter.

"Don't you remember the book you gave me as a boy?" I asked him, disappointed in his response to my cue. "The one on the excavations at Angkor?" He riffled through the memory of a lifetime of books he had bestowed on friends and family. Then his face lit up, and he harrumphed, "Oh, yes. Angkor, the Malcolm MacDonald book, the one with the sculptures of the Temple of the Leper King on the cover." He paused to consider the possibilities of our traveling together, then painfully readjusted himself in his old leather reading chair.

"I just wish I were as confident as you that I was going to recover," he said with the first note of despair I'd ever heard from him. "Of course, I'd like to see these places with you. It would be wonderful."

Then his voice broke. "But I don't know, son, if I'm going to make it."

No one I've ever met has pronounced the word "wonderful" like my father. He stressed the first syllable, "won," as if the adjective did indeed have its roots in victory and triumph. He so rarely used upbeat words, so when he did I knew he meant it. Hearing it there and then, watching this once-ferocious and formidable man sit in a chair, unable to move his hands and feet because of a crippling nerve disease, I was shaken. Still, I feigned confidence and courage and promised we would hit the road together as soon as he recovered.

He didn't. Four months later, on the very Ides of March which he had announced every year in our house as though it were the strangest day on the calendar, my father died in his sleep.

Shortly after the funeral, while packing up the books in his stilled apartment, I made one of the few vows in my life. I promised myself I would take the journey for both of us, make the pilgrimage to a place made holy by the play of light on stone and the devotion of pilgrims who had walked astonishing distances so that they might touch the sacred sculpture and offer their prayers on the wings of incense.

And, in so doing, perhaps restore my faith in life itself.

Phil Cousineau's peripatetic career has included stints as a sports-writer, playing basketball in Europe, harvesting date trees on an Israeli kibbutz, painting forty-four Victorian houses in San Francisco, and leading adventure travel tours around the world. He is the author of several books, including The Art of Pilgrimage: The Seeker's Guide to Making Travel Sacred, *from which this story was ex-cerpted. He grew up in Wayne, Michigan, and lives with his family in San Francisco.*

FREDDA ROSEN

✦ ✦ ✦

Shalom, Bombay

All religions have a home in the cauldron
of spirituality that is India.

TO KNOW INDIA IS TO HEAR HER. VILLAGE ROADS AND CITY
streets are stuffed with people and their transport. Horns
blare, engines cough. People shout, people scream. I was in
Bombay, and I'd been away from home too long. I had a
headache from India.

I also had too many hours to wait for my flight home. I'd
already seen the Hanging Gardens and shopped myself silly.
But I didn't have a gift for my father.

"There's a synagogue in Bombay," he had told me when I
left for India. I smiled and ignored the implication. My father
has been trying to get me into a synagogue since I left Beth
El Academy in 1964. I've had other things to do. But now I
shrugged.

"Got nothing else today," I thought. I figured there would
be a synagogue gift shop like the one at Beth El, and I'd get
him something there.

A local businessman I met at the airport wrote the directions:

"Jewish Temple, near Byculla Bridge, opposite Richardson and Crudder, Ltd."

Kuldeep, my driver for the day, scrutinized the paper.

"Many temples in Bombay," he said.

"Not Hindu temple," I said. "Jewish temple. Synagogue."

He gave me a blank look, but shifted into gear. We added our horn to the honks and screeches of the city streets.

The sun followed us, searing through the car windows, making my clothes stick to my body. My head reverberated as we crossed a bridge labeled Byculla. Kuldeep braked in front of a snack bar, and consulted in Hindi with the owner and two customers. Arms waived to the left and right.

Kuldeep took off down a tiny alley, scattering chickens and children. He drove through the dirt yard of an apartment complex, turned again, and pulled up in front of a large stone structure.

He looked around and gave me a grin. I sighed. The building was topped with a huge cross.

"Place for Catholics," he said.

I took a deep breath. "Jewish," I said. "Not Catholic, Jewish."

We began again, asking at a tailor's shop, stopping a schoolboy. Kuldeep honked through cars, buses, trucks, and bikes. The air was thick with incense, carbon monoxide, and wood smoke. Two aspirins did nothing for my headache or my spirits. We found no synagogues.

We did find a police station.

"Anyone speak English?" My voice was plaintive.

Khaki-suited men gave me the once over. One took the paper I waved and studied it.

"Synagogue," I said hopefully. "Jewish temple."

The policeman brightened. "Oh," he said. "You want Jain temple!"

I stifled a hiss and tried a new tact. "Where is Richardson and Crudder? Richardson and Crudder, Ltd.?"

He told Kuldeep, and we entered the fray once more. This time we scored. Kuldeep found the offices of Richardson and Crudder. I looked across the clogged avenue and saw a two-story building. It was adorned with a six-pointed star. A sign proclaimed Magen David.

"There it is!" I pointed.

Kuldeep responded with an Indian U-turn: a maneuver that involves crossing four lanes of moving traffic and staccato bursts of the horn. He pulled up to the synagogue entrance. Near the gate, a family had set up housekeeping. A woman chopped vegetables, her son washed his hair. They stared at me as I walked inside.

So did the three gray-haired men who sat on the porch of the synagogue. They were small and brown and wore skull caps. I introduced myself.

"Abraham," said one of the men. He waved at the others. "He's Abraham, too. And Ephraim."

They each gave me a smile that revealed missing teeth.

"You want to see the *safers*?" the first Abraham asked, referring to the Torahs, the sacred scrolls.

They ushered me inside the synagogue. Abraham pointed to two plaques. One commemorated the one hundredth anniversary of the synagogue, the other touted a donation from a couple from Great Neck, New York. There wasn't a gift shop in sight.

The sanctuary was lined with simple wooden pews. In the center was a raised platform with two gilded chairs. It was cool and quiet. I heard horns, but they were far in the distance.

Ephraim waved toward a corner where men worked on a scaffolding. He told me in careful English that the synagogue, which is over 120 years old, was being restored. But few people worship here now. Ephraim said they rarely have the ten men required to hold a service.

"We don't make *minyan* much. Sometimes on Saturday," he said.

The other Abraham told me that there are only six or seven thousand Jews in India. "We got the Torah from England," he said.

He opened the door to the arc, touched my hand, and motioned to the Torahs. They had embroidered velvet covers like the ones at home, at Beth El. I ran my fingers over the soft fabric. Then I remembered. I raised my hand to my lips, just as I'd been taught in Hebrew school. The three men lifted their heads and smiled. I noticed that my headache was gone, but my eyes were wet.

I blinked, and told them that I wanted to make a donation to the restoration work. "In honor of my father," I said.

I signed over a traveler's check. The men passed it among themselves, turning it over and over. Kuldeep, who had joined us, explained in Hindi how to cash it.

Abraham pressed my hand. "I give you my card," he said. He gave me a paper with the synagogue address stamped on it.

"Pictures?" I asked, taking out my camera.

"Oh, yes," Ephraim said.

I took one of the three men standing at the entrance to the sanctuary. Kuldeep took one of me in front of the synagogue. I made a mental note to have it framed as a gift for my father.

After all, his errand had brought me a gift, too. The Abrahams and Ephraim shook my hand as I left.

"See you at home, in Jerusalem," Ephraim said. "Peace be with you."

And it was.

Fredda Rosen has written for many U.S. newspapers and magazines and contributed a series of profiles to A Woman's Place Is Everywhere. *She lives in New York.*

JAN HAAG

✦ ✦ ✦

Mission Walk

An old California mission is a modern miracle.

I HAD FIVE EXTRA DAYS, SO I DECIDED TO WALK DOWN
California's Salinas Valley. I started at the Soledad Mission,
walked down the blazing summer valley, and spent the first
night atop Pine Canyon in the crystal-clear night air.

At the side of the road just behind a private gate high above
King City, I laid out my sleeping equipment—two emergency
blankets that fold into three-inch squares. It was the first night
I had ever slept by myself, all alone, beneath the stars. It was a
night of ecstatic pleasure in sights and sounds: the lights of the
valley miles below me, the leaves rustling in the slightest
breeze, the noises of nocturnal animals, and the road was so
hard that I probably didn't sleep more than twenty minutes.

The owner of the private gate, wearing a ten-gallon hat and
cowboy boots, discovered me in the dark on his property.
"You scared my wife!" he said. Then, finding I was just a
harmless gray-haired lady, he told me how to find the road
that would lead me down to Mission San Antonio which lies
in the middle of the Hunter-Liggett military base.

In the morning as I finished packing my sleeping gear, my host drove up again in his pickup with some water. I had asked him in the night where to find water in the morning and he gave me directions so complicated that I was sure I'd never find the spring. Thankful, I drank and drank from his huge canteen and filled my plastic water bottle. Then he pointed me down the road which led directly into Hunter-Liggett, along which, he cautioned, I would find 100 unmarked dirt roads built for practice maneuvers, where the army could prepare for war.

"Stay to the right," he said, "every time you come to a main crossroads. Once down in the valley, go left, the mission is south."

I thanked him profusely and walked away into the dawn.

The top of the road was flat and ran through thick pines, then it began a steep decline. It went down and down and down and down and down and down for, perhaps, ten miles. Having taken off my sandals, as I often do in India, what a joy it was to walk effortlessly downhill, alone, through the silk-soft dirt. The trees changed to sycamores; narrow dirt roads disappeared in all directions, over every mound and around many trees. There was not a single person or habitation to be seen. One huge commercial plane passed overhead, going north, so high I could barely hear its sound. Farther along I came to an old corral with a wooden water tank, dry, cracked, and askew on its high stilts. The vegetation became sparser as I approached the valley floor where the baked dust and rocks fairly shimmered with the heat. I drank more thirstily of my gift-given water.

At the main crossroad on the valley floor, I turned left, but I had no idea how far away the mission lay. I walked for another hour. A single car came by on that dirt road, going north. The woman driving, who was not at all surprised to see

me, assured me the mission was in the direction I was going—
she didn't know how far. It was as if she often saw straw-hatted
women with small orange backpacks ambling along her route.

"Is there any water between here and there?"

"I don't know." As the car moved slowly up the road, puffs
of dust rose behind her tires. "Good luck," she called.

Noon approached. The heat grew more intense. My water
was almost gone. Men, I had already begun to learn, weren't
so insouciant about water. The next day I was to be repeatedly
warned by men from passing cars that I was walking in the
worst heat wave the Salinas Valley had ever known, and several would insist on transporting me from shade point to shade
point. But that was later.

At the moment, how confident it made me feel not to be
warned by the woman driver about the possible dire consequences of my walk. The Spanish had traversed the unmarked
land in the seventeenth century, and she and I saw nothing
odd about a walk along known roads in the twentieth.

As I continued, nothing but acres of sage and bits of chap-
arral met my gaze. The dazzle of the bone-dry air made me
squint and filled me with delight. Could I make my water
last? I watched this interesting thought turn from a movie-
like image of prospectors lost in the desert, to amusement, to
wonder, to concern, to worry. Then I began to take deep
breaths as it touched, ever so slightly, on uncivilized fear. For
it seemed no matter what judiciously bird-like sips I took,
the water disappeared as if I was boiling it on a high flame.
Nor did my sparing efforts allow me even once to slake my
thirst. The sun rose higher and turned white. I was wearing
my sandals now, for the hard dirt was too hot to touch with
my bare feet.

Then, as if in answer to my requirement for a miracle, taller and taller, almost bamboo-like trees began to appear on my left. I saw a cow.

Trees? Cow? There must be water.

I quickened my pace. A little farther on I stepped off the road. Within minutes I found a running stream. It not only supplied me with water to drink, but a cool bath and a gourmet lunch of fresh watercress. I rinsed my blue necker-chief blouse, and put it on dripping wet to set off again for the mission.

Another half-hour down the road I met a man jogging in the noon day heat. How could anyone jog in such weather? He must, I guessed, be a soldier not far from home. God him-self, I decided, must be keeping an eye on this particular spar-row, for already I'd drunk half my new bottle of stream water, and the heat had began to patina my legs with white powder. It was as if the water in my system were evaporating so fast that it left salt on my surface. The jogger assured me, without slacking his pace, that my goal was just ahead.

Across a bridge over a dry course and beyond some plat-inum-colored grassy mounds lay one of California's most beautiful missions. I approached its dusty, creamy stucco exte-rior as if I had arrived at the gates of heaven. Huge carved doors opened into a high-vaulted church which was dark, deserted, and very cool. It was like plunging into a secret pool deep within the earth which seemed to hold only the dark-ness, the coolness, and the friendly, if ghostly, flickering of votive candles.

Slowly my eyes adjusted. I gazed for a long time at the aged pigments of the altar, the designs along the walls that the Indians had painted. Though I had heard nothing but my own footsteps and the call of a bird or two most of the morning, still I was entranced by the utter silence the church offered, and grateful for shelter from the blazing sun. I speculated on how soon I would be able to walk on in the heat, how far I would get that day. After all, it was just past noon. Then I closed my eyes and allowed myself to dream.

Longingly I thought, Oh, if only these were the old days. If only I were a real pilgrim during the time the California missions had flourished. If only I were a traveler of 200 years ago—with news from Soledad or San Francisco, the Presidio, maybe, or from Spain—how they would welcome me, how they would rejoice at my coming, as people still do in parts of Asia. For in many countries, to this day, the guest is considered to be God. Any guest or stranger's coming is looked upon as a rare and wonderful event. In the old days the missionaries would have offered me hospitality, a bed, food. They would have urged me to stay, urged me to talk. I would have told them such stories!

After awhile I stepped from the cool darkness of the sanctuary into the courtyard. The sun poured its white, hot light down on a central rose garden enclosed by a columned and roofed arcade. A fountain, to which spoked paths led, splashed in the middle. I chose a shaded wooden bench and put down my pack. From it I took my needlepoint and began to stitch. I always carry a piece of needlepoint; it is my form of meditation. I use them as diaries, incorporating into their designs patterns I find along the way. The finished works, which resemble small Oriental rugs, remind me of my earthly and spiritual journeys.

In the shade it was just a little more than pleasantly warm. I stitched, working a blue-and-brown border around a central motif of the Tibetan Kundalini symbol. In the garden, a young man worked around the base of the roses, cultivating, weeding, snipping the withered blooms. His movement was the only movement in the breathless heat. After a while a woman

came to sit on another wooden bench under the shade of the
arcade some distance from me.

When the young man finished his work with the roses,
he gathered the clippings, put away his tools, and paused to
speak to the other woman. Then he walked soundlessly toward me down the terra-cotta tiles of the arcade. He was
dressed in blue jeans and a blue shirt; his hair was blond. He
stopped beside my bench and looked at me. His eyes were
dark, yet reflected the blue of the sky and, even before he
spoke, I was awed by the depth of their compassion. He said
to me as if he were continuing a conversation, "And where
have you come from?"

I said rather breathlessly, perhaps a little proudly, and certainly feeling like the impostor of a pilgrim: "I just walked
over from the Soledad Mission." (In case you are not familiar
with the terrain, there is a distance of about thirty miles
between each of the twenty-one missions; they were one day's
ride by horse from each other along El Camino Real from
San Diego to Sonoma. Years later, now, when I have more
humor, I find myself smiling. I realize what an amazing statement that must have been from a middle-aged woman in the
100-degree heat in the courtyard of the remotest mission of
them all, where, very probably, no one had walked in from a
neighboring mission in the last 100 years.)

"Oh, you must be tired," this kind young man said with
total, unquestioning belief and enormous sympathy. "Would
you like a shower?"

"Oh yes!" I fairly gasped.

He smiled. "Would you like to stay the night?"

"Oh yes!"

My ability to believe in miracles took a quantum leap.

It turned out—a fact I had not known—that Mission San
Antonio was a functioning mission run by the Franciscans.

The young man in the blue jeans with the dark eyes bluer than the heavens, bluer than Michelangelo's cerulean blue skies, was a Franciscan brother. He showed me to a small cell in the women's cloisters and invited me to supper in the refectory. The room held a narrow bed, a desk, a chair, a small old-fashioned wardrobe, and a casement window embedded in the two-foot thick walls. This window looked out on the platinum-and-gold fields, studded here and there with live oaks, a landscape so beautiful one could not doubt it was designed by God for his padres. I washed the clothes I had been wearing and showered in the women's bathroom. I rested, read a little, and put in a few more stitches.

At supper, the food was abundant, but not my kind of fare: boiled cabbage, ham, potatoes, with applesauce for desert. And I was not, as I never am when I walk, very hungry. I carried only dried figs and almonds, and ate along the road only what I could glean: wild berries, a tomato left in the harvested fields, one green pepper—nothing I felt that anyone would begrudge me.

There were several brothers at the table, and the old priest—Irish, I guessed—who had a florid complexion, was gracious, and talked of all the worldly subjects about which I could not—living as I was that evening in the richness of the miraculous—utter a single word. The young man with the loving eyes was dressed now, like the others, in a brown and cowled homespun robe. He asked me my story, how I happened to be walking from the Soledad Mission to San Antonio. I hesitantly spoke of my interest in pilgrimage, how it was my desire to walk around the world. I did not tell them my practice and religious interest at that time was mostly in Eastern meditation, the Hindu tradition. They invited me to attend early morning Mass in the small chapel. I said I had to start walking very early in the morning because it would get too hot soon after sunrise, but I would come to Mass if I could. They reminded me that San Miguel was the next stop down on the mission trail.

Looking out at the stars that gleamed beyond the window embedded in the deep, thick walls, I rested that night in the delight of a wish granted. Rising early, I packed and went, even before Mass, to leave a little gift of some figs and almonds on the kitchen table. I attended Mass and left as quickly as I could, but not quickly enough to avoid a kindly invitation to breakfast, which I declined. I stepped into the dark church, left a coin, and lighted a votive candle. My heart was almost breaking with bliss for the sweetness of the miracle that had granted me my pilgrim's wish when I had first sat in the darkened church. Then I stepped out the great front doors.

There, to meet me on the steps, was the young brother in his brown robes, again inviting me to breakfast. Again I declined, saying I must go because already it was getting hot. It was nearly nine o'clock. I could feel in the heat the promise of a blistering day.

Then, to my heart-stopping astonishment, the young Franciscan, whom I had learned from the other woman was called Brother Joachim, knelt. Extending a tender and gentle hand, he touched my feet, saying, "But your feet are blistered."

Which was true. I was wearing rubber zoris and great pockets of fluid had formed on the insides of my big toes. But the blisters did not hurt. I felt them not at all. However, I had, late yesterday afternoon, mentioned them to the other woman. She must have mentioned them to the brother.

"But they do not hurt at all," I assured him, "And truly, I must be going or it will be too hot to walk."

He touched my feet again. I felt it as a blessing. As he stood up, he said, "What can I give you? I must give you something." Out of a few moments search of his habit, he found a Saint Christopher medal of red plastic. "Take this," he said.

I did. I walked away as a pilgrim who had been blessed.

Nowhere in all my spiritual pilgrimage have I ever again seen eyes so full of grace and love as those of the young Franciscan, Brother Joachim.

Jan Haag is a travel writer, novelist, poet, and former Director of National Production Programs for the American Film Institute. She has lived and studied in India, China, Thailand, Nepal, Russia, and Mexico.

The Garden of Immortality

*In 1921, a young man invaded
the sanctum of a ghost.*

IT WAS ALMOST NIGHT, AND THE FIRST SHY BREEZE WE HAD felt that day came from the Jumna. Across the river, through the twilight haze, a huge and swelling dome could be dimly distinguished from the dark sky behind. Soaring from the treetops into a bank of clouds, it seemed a Maxfield Parrish picture come to life.

"What's that?" I asked of Ahmed, my Punjabi companion.

"That the Taj Mahal."

Had it been the post office or the mission church he could not have spoken with less enthusiasm, yet it would be impossible to describe how deeply I was stirred by this casual reply. It was as if Columbus on his first voyage had asked Roderigo: "What's that dark line over there?" and Roderigo had answered: "Oh, that? That's land."

The Taj Mahal had been deified in my mind ever since that childhood day when I had first looked upon an oil painting of the fairy tomb and read the immortal story of its creation. It had always been a dream castle to me, something so fabulous it could not have dimensions and weight and location; something so lovely it could not exist outside of picture books. Poring for hours at a time over these very books I had come to revere this building above all others, and had made a divinity out of Arjemand, the Mogul princess who became the Empress Mumtaz Mahal, whose beauty and perfection it commemorates. All my adventures in India up to this time I had known to be only preludes to the great final adventure—the actual sight and touch of the Taj.

Facts and legends came to me now in a jumbled mass, as I stood in the fortress tower and watched the great dome disappear into the night. The follies of the Emperor Shah Jehan, who built the Taj, were forgotten; what mattered the number of his crimes—his genius as a builder, his fame as the greatest lover in history, were more worthy of memory. In the marble poetry of the Taj this greatest lover has immortalized the object of his passion. Arjemand, favorite among a thousand wives, is embodied in its stones; her chastity is carved into its spotless walls; her exquisiteness reproduced in every delicate line; her majesty reflected in the aereal grace of dome and minaret that floated and faded there above the river side.

We had been silent for some moments, enjoying the coolness of the night that now had blotted out the distance. Ahmed was the first to speak:

"You know Shah Jehan?"

"Yes." I said, "I 'know' him."

"He die here in balcony."

"What, Ahmed! Is this the Jasmine Tower?"

He assured me it was, and that we were treading thoughtlessly on stones numbered among the most hallowed in India, for this was the point from which the emperor last saw his beloved wife's memorial. For her shrine he had squandered the wealth of an empire, until his subjects, led by his own son, revolted and imprisoned the "King of Earth" here in his own palace, on the banks of the Jumna. Dethroned, disgraced, held captive, for seven years he had only the memory of his lovely Arjemand to comfort him. At last, when he felt his end was near, the old and broken man pleaded, not in vain, to be carried at dawn to the Jasmine Tower, where his dying eyes might rest upon the distant minarets of the mausoleum. There his heart and soul already were, there he knew his body was soon to be, beside her for whom he had created the one perfect thing. Through fading eyes he watched the eastern horizon brighten with light, watched the first beam of sunrise strike the dome. Then the heavy weary gates closed forever—and the Taj passed from view.

"You stay here all night, Sahib?"

"No," I said, my reverie broken, "I am ready to go now."

We descended from the tower, threaded our way out of the unlit corridors, found the grim entrance gate, and hurried homeward through the animated streets. But I saw neither the swinging lanterns, nor the shops, nor the crowds. My thoughts were of Mumtaz Mahal, whom, on the morrow, I planned to meet, at last, face to face.

Early and eagerly the next morning I set forth alone. I passed beneath the ruddy arch that commands entrance to the gardens of the Taj, and there, behold!—beyond, in the blinding summer sunshine I saw it, a miracle of sky and verdure and ivory, beckoning to me through the framing gateway. My dream castle had come to life.

I answered its call with absolute surrender, moving almost without volition down the marble pavement that led straight and glittering into its very heart. I was unaware of the fountains at my feet, or of the indigo sky above. I saw only my long-sought Taj awaiting me, harmonious as music, lovely as the face of the immortal woman it commemorates.

The entire day I remained beside the snowy temple, enchanted by its serenity, forgetful of time and self. I wandered about its polished corridors, climbed upon its roof, descended into its crypts. Attracted by a myriad of colors I drifted about the gardens that enthrone the monster pearl, tarried by the lily pools reflecting dome and minaret, and loitered along the avenue of stately cypresses.

Noon came, and afternoon. From a shaded bed of grass I looked up at the shimmering walls. Built of cold stone they are, and yet how ethereal; erected by man, yet touched by the gods. "Make it as beautiful as she was beautiful, as delicate, as graceful," commanded the grief-striken emperor of Ustad Isa, his greatest architect. "Make it the image and the soul of her beauty." And in a dream Ustad Isa visioned a finished tomb that was as lovely yet withal as majestic as the moon-faced empress. Though two hundred and fourscore years have passed since this dream was realized and Mumtaz Mahal laid to rest, today the Taj appears to have been built but yesterday. There it floated above me, not only a symbol of matchless feminine beauty but an expression of the adoration the Shah-in-Shah felt for his chosen favorite of all the palace. Even in building, it was marked by the passion that distinguished the idyllic union of the emperor and the Lady Arjemand, for he spent upon it not only his treasures, but his grief and his tears. Thus it has come to pass that the sepulcher has a soul, which, so legends tell, has been known to manifest itself on summer nights, and in the image of the queen emerge in radiance from the tomb, dissolved to mist by moonbeams.

Twilight came, and the wind ceased. The tropical dark blue background of all this beauty was fading into night. About me the deserted gardens were hushed except for the faint splash of falling water. Twilight faded into starlight. Still I clung to my veiled Taj, and no duty or need could lure me away from this glimpse into Paradise.

The summer moon had reached its zenith a week before, and now, rapidly waning, rose nearer the hour of dawn than darkness. Yet at midnight every visitor must depart from the gardens, so I would have to leave without seeing the palace melt beneath the flood of moonlight. Already guards were closing the tower gates; sentries were gathering before the threshold of the tomb. A few belated stragglers were being hurried to their waiting gharries, and as I saw them go the thought came to me: "Why not try to stay?—then I could possess the Taj by myself alone!" The romantic possibilities of such an adventure captivated my fancy. Quickly I hid in a darkened grove. The watchmen, carrying their lamps, came close to me—but passed on. Not for a kingdom would I have surrendered, with this opportunity before me to remain through the night by the side of my marble mistress.

Then from the entrance I heard the ponderous iron-bound doors groan as they were swung laboriously into place. I heard the clank of fastening chains, and their ominous echo, reverberating from wall to wall across the breathless garden, filled me with sudden dread, for I, a mortal, was now imprisoned with a pale pearl ghost—I was alone with the Taj Mahal.

For an hour, and an hour more, waiting for the moon, I lingered patiently beneath my willow grove, enraptured by the dim beauty of this dreamland and by its hovering mystery. Then with the tolling of two the shroud was lifted from the sky, as the moon glinted through the boughs upon the sleeping garden.

Utter silence had reigned till now; but all at once from a top-most branch came the herald hooting of a sentinel owl, commanding the myriad invisible inhabitants of the garden to awake from bush and vine and flower, to acclaim their lady of the night. Straightway a cricket orchestra began to chirrup forth its homage; flying-foxes tumbled through the air. From flame-of-the-forest and banyan bough, from clematis vine and honeysuckle tangles, came stirs and flutters of awakened doves and the faint woodnote of the *hoopee*. Only the guardsmen at the gateway slumbered on.

Then, as I watched, the moon floated upward from the trees to commune in secret with the phantom Taj, while all earthly worshipers were far away and the union safe from the disenchanting gaze of mortals. Silvered, the mausoleum emerged from shadow, and hypnotic in new radiance beckoned to me once more. Heedless of consequences I crept from my green grotto—there was no sound. On tiptoe I mounted a stairway to the dais—there was no challenge, for the sentries had been touched by magic too, and slept profoundly.

Higher rose the moon; fairer gleamed the Taj, a harmonious pile of masonry in the sunshine of the morning, a specter underneath the stars, now transfigured to a gleaming gossamer, an airy bubble that might evaporate into ether while one looked upon it.

Unaware of the passing moments, I watched the shadows move in the deep recesses of the façade, until unable to resist the lure of the interior, I turned to the main portal. Stealthily I crept around the sleeping sentries, softly crossed the threshold, and entering stood beside the faint-lit tombs of the Shah-in-Shah and Arjemand. A bronze lantern hung by a chain from the obscurity of the dome above, and the light shining through its perforated sides cast fantastic shadows on the carven walls. Forgetful of sentries, I whistled a subdued note and listened to it ringing and re-ringing in slowly dying echoes far up in the blackness of the vault.

The fourth hour came, and found me standing pensive beside the Empress' grave. A pilgrim to her shrine, she had blessed me with protection. With sudden shame I realized I had brought no offering. Neither gold nor silver did I have, not even a flower; but in a recess of my wallet, kept for memory's sake, there withered a twig of myrtle, plucked six months past from some courtyard in the Alhambra of the Moors, amid whose storied battlements I had sought romance on such a night as this. From one Moslem monument in Spain it had come to another in India, directed perhaps by the hand of Allah. Reverently I placed these fragile leaves upon her tomb. The wind brushed gently through the vaulted corridors, and slowly swung the hanging lantern to and fro; and I was filled with happiness, fancying that her spirit had sent this murmured benediction.

No one was awake to see me creep forth into the balmy night, or to watch my shadow as it left the marble platform and moved again across the moon-blanched park. Streams of water from the Jumna flowed upon the thirsty gardens, so that a glittering film covered lawn and bed and pavement. Barefoot, I waded in the flowered ponds. How cool and refreshing was the touch of flooded grass—how far from the realities of earth I felt myself. On a marble bench I sat beside the deepest lily pool and looked at the great white blossoms drifting among the reflected stars of an Indian sky. And as I looked there seemed to come from its depths a call, the same that had twice drawn me powerless into the Taj: "Come to my caress, oh, mortal—bathe your body in my coolness— float upon my tranquil mirror—wash your mind of consciousness."

Only an insomniac owl watched me remove my clothes, or heard the faint ripple as I dropped into the alabaster pool. This was a page from the *Arabian Nights*, a reversion to the fabled luxury of ancient emperors—this, at last, was Romance.

It was but an hour before dawn. The moon had reached the peak of its course and was shining with unearthly brilliance. Alone, in all this supernatural beauty, resting by the pool before the phantom Taj, I felt myself transported to some previous existence that knew neither time nor space nor substance. I and all that I beheld was myth. The subconscious mind was master, linking me with previous incarnations in the dim past.

A strange ecstasy came to me. I heard myself laugh deliriously. A giant lily floated on the unruffled mirror, and as I leaned over the alabaster rim to tear it from its stem—whose eerie face peered back at me from the water, whose queer slant eyes, whose horns? In terror I leaped to my feet. Was it this that I had been in the beginning, or was it to this that I had come, distorted by some avenging spirit for profaning with my touch a sanctuary of immortality?

Caw—caw—caw! A crow in a nearby grove mocked my bewilderment. Twice startled, I glanced up to find day streaking the east. There was a rush of wind, a rustle of leaves…. Suddenly I was aware of being bitterly cold. Realities began to emerge before my eyes. The gardens lay about me, stark and tangible. The Taj—had turned again—to stone.

In a fever of dread and perplexity I flung on my clothes, hurried to the tower gate, surrendering myself to the sentries, and besought them to liberate me from this realm of the supernatural.

As I passed, with a guard on either side, underneath the vaulted tower, I looked back through the arch-framed opening to find the sky in amber hues, the park dew-pearled, waking to the matin song of lark and oriole. I saw the Taj, reflecting the rose-and-gold horizon, still tenderly beautiful, still beckoning, and as I turned to her for one last, farewell glimpse, the first beam of sunrise struck the dome. Then the heavy weary gates closed behind me, and the Lady of my Dreams passed from view.

Richard Halliburton was a world traveler who wrote numerous books in his short lifetime, including The Glorious Adventure, *the* Complete Book of Marvels, *and* The Royal Road to Romance, *from which this story was excerpted. Halliburton is known for having paid the lowest toll to cross the Panama Canal, which he swam in 1928, paying thirty-six cents. Born in Tennessee in 1900, he died in 1939 as he and his crew attempted to sail a Chinese junk, the* Sea Dragon, *from Hong Kong to San Francisco.*

PART THREE

MYSTERY

LAURIE GOUGH

* * *

Naxos Nights

A traveler from the cold north
has an enigmatic encounter.

NO SINGLE INCIDENT IN MY LIFE HAS BEEN SO STRANGE, SO
hard to grasp, so totally lacking in feasible explanation. I came
to Naxos by mistake, but maybe there are no mistakes. Maybe
sometimes we're meant to be led here and there, to certain
places at certain times for reasons beyond our understanding,
beyond our will or the spell of the moon or the arrangement
of the stars in the sky. Maybe all the dark and eternal nameless
things lurking around us have their own purpose and vision
for us. Who knows?

When I was twenty-three, I was traveling alone through
Europe. I'd been in the rain for two months in Britain and
discovered I didn't like being wet. I wanted to dry out and
perhaps I wanted more than that—an inner light, a deeper
understanding of life's complexities, a friend. With all those
rainy days traveling alone, a fire had been extinguished within
me and I needed rekindling. One morning I woke up soggy.
I was on a beach in Scotland at the time, so soggy was to be

expected, but I was also shivering and miserable. I decided to escape to Greece as fast as possible.

Three days later I was on a midnight flight to Athens. At six in the morning, dragging my sleepless, jet-lagged body around the port of Piraeus, I came to a clapboard sign of a ferry schedule for various Greek islands. I was still dripping wet psychologically and dead tired, but I wanted things: a beach, the sun, a warm dry place to sleep, a Greek salad. I bought a ticket for the island of Paros because the ferry was leaving in ten minutes. Arbitrary, yes, but I was young and still arranged my life that way. Six hours later we pulled into the Paros harbor. From the wooden bench on the boat where I'd been napping, I looked up to see a jammed crowd of passengers swarming the exit doors. Since I was groggy and exhausted, I decided to stay on the bench a few more minutes and let the crowd disappear. When I looked up again, in what seemed just a few minutes, I was appalled to see the boat pulling away from the harbor, the passengers all gone, and me left alone on the boat. For the next two hours I worried we were sailing back to Athens, and I was too embarrassed to ask the men who worked on the ferry about it.

Fortunately, in two hours we arrived at another island. I got off the boat on the island of Naxos and walked with my backpack along the dock where I was immediately swarmed by a sea of short, round, middle-aged women in polyester black dresses and black socks who wanted me to stay at their guest houses and sleep on their roofs. Assuming the roles of foreign eccentric aunts, they took my arms and patted my hands, trying to pull me into their lives, their doughy bodies.

I didn't go to the houses of any of those women. In the recesses of my drowsy mind I remembered I needed a beach, and sleep. Leaving the busy little port town behind, I headed south along the beach, walking for a long time through scatterings of bodies lying on the white sand, topless French women playing frisbee, nut-brown boys throwing balls, incoming waves and *tavernas* off to the side. A pure Aegean light fell on my head like a bleached curtain draping from the sky. It was a lean and haunting landscape, savagely dry, yet the light was uncannily clear with a blue sky big enough to crack open the world, had the world been a giant egg. The crowds thinned as I walked farther along the beach and music from the *taverna* faded in the distance. Finally, I spotted something under the shade of an olive grove—a small bamboo wind shelter that someone must have constructed and recently abandoned. Perfect. I'd found the place to drop down and sleep. And, although I didn't know it at the time, I'd found the place that would become my home for over a month.

I slept the rest of that day in the bamboo wind shelter under the olive grove and when I woke up it was dark and all the people were gone. A night wind danced across my face and shooting stars crashed across the sky. I ran along the beach, delirious, exalted, and finally dry.

My days on the beach took on their own rhythm. In the morning, rose rays of sunrise from behind a dark mountain would wake me, and if they didn't, the island's omnipresent roosters would. The sea would be calm at dawn and I'd go for a swim before the day's beach crowd arrived. Walking back to my bamboo shelter I'd say hello and chat with the smiling waiter, Nikos, at the nearby *taverna* as he set out his chairs for the day's customers. Nikos was handsome in the way many Greek men are handsome, which has more to do with the way they look at you than how they themselves look. Nikos was good at looking rather than good-looking, which was almost the same thing in the end. When the sun got too high I'd escape its burning rays and read books in the shade of my olive grove. I'm a redhead—an absolute curse in a desert like

Greece. The waves would gather momentum as the day passed and at some point every afternoon they would be at their fullest. That's when the old men would appear. From seemingly out of nowhere, a gathering of weathered, mahogany Greek men with sunken chests and black bathing shorts would converge to stand on the shore and survey the sea. The Aegean in dark-blue spasms would be reaching its zenith there in the afternoon light and, from my olive grove, I'd watch it also. The old men would enter the sea together, simultaneously turn to face the shore, and hunch over with their knees slightly bent, skinny arms outstretched, waiting. They'd look over their shoulders at the ocean beyond, ready to jump up and join in at precisely the right moment. They always knew when that was. I would join them and always laughed when riding the waves, but I never saw those men crack a smile. I decided that when I was eighty I would take the waves that seriously also. After that many years of life on earth, what could be more important than playing in the waves?

Sometimes I'd walk into town to explore, buy fruit and bottled water, and watch old men argue politics over their Turkish coffee served in tiny cups. The coffee was sweet and strong and one-third full of gooey sediment. At sunset the men would turn their chairs to face the sun as it melted the day into the sea. They'd sigh and drink their ouzo or *citron* or *kitro*—a specialty of Naxos, lemon liqueur—and stop talking until the sky drained of color. Parish priests with stovepipe hats, long robes, and beards would stroll the narrow alleys with their hands behind their backs looking exactly like movie extras. Old women in black would watch me as I passed, ask me about snow occasionally. I'd wander through the maze of whitewashed houses, the stark lines of white and blue, and stumble back home over the rocky land of dry absolutes in a heady daze. Nothing is murky in Greece, nor hazy, nor humid, nor dewy. Lush doesn't live there. Greece is a rock garden of shrubs and laurel, juniper and cypress, thyme and oregano. Wildflowers spin colors that surge out of a pure clarity and in this clarity the forms of things are finer. Greece shimmers from afar, is hardy in the distance, and chill beneath your bones. In the dry heat of this arid place, donkeys sound-off at all hours, as if agitated. They'd wake me even in the dead of night.

One evening at sunset a man on a moped zipped by as I was walking along the beach. He came to a stop in the sand ahead and turned to ask my name. I'd seen him before at the *taverna*, throwing his head back to laugh when Nikos the waiter told jokes. The man on the moped offered me a ride down the beach and I took it. Naxos has one entire uninterrupted beach and in twenty minutes or so we came to his village, a cluster of houses and an outdoor restaurant overlooking the sea. The man let me off, smiled without speaking and disappeared. I went to the restaurant for dinner and chatted with some tourists. We didn't say anything significant. Mostly we watched the sky, which by then was blood-red cracked apart with silver shots of whisky. Shortly after I found a bus that took me back to the town of Naxos.

By the time I finally arrived at the olive grove it was dark except for the light of the moon heaving itself full over the mountain. I came to my bamboo wind shelter and found it creaking in the wind, desolate, as it was the day I arrived, abandoned by its inhabitant. My backpack and the little home I'd made with my sleeping bag and pillows were gone, taken. For approximately three seconds I felt a panic spread through me, which didn't seem healthy, so I looked at the moon and seeing that dependable milky rock hovering up there like the planet's eccentric uncle made me smile, and I remembered that in the great scheme of the universe, this kind of thing didn't matter. I had my money, traveler's checks, and passport with me and could buy the few things I needed. My backpack had been too heavy anyway, and traveling light would be a relief, a new challenge, something to write home about in postcards. Sitting on the sand I thought of the stolen things I would miss: my journal, my camera, some foreign change, a pair of Levi's, my toothbrush, my shoes. My shoes!

I fell asleep surprisingly quickly under the full moon that night. Luckily the thieves hadn't stolen the floor of the wind shelter—the bamboo mats—and I was comfortable and warm, but an hour or so later a group of hysterical German women came and woke me. They'd been staying at a campground down the beach and they too had been victims of an annoying petty crime. Standing with them was a quiet, tall Dutch man with a blond beard and thick glasses. His belongings had been stolen also, even an expensive camera was gone, but I noticed that, unlike the women, he wasn't the least perturbed by it. In fact he was calm, even amused, and I felt an instant affinity for this unusual man. In the midst of the German panic, three Scottish backpackers came along and asked if this was a safe place to camp. I laughed, which seemed to irritate the German women, while Martin, the Dutch man, said it was safe except for the occasional theft in the area, but really quite peaceful during the day. The German women went off to search for clues down the beach. Martin and I lay back on the sand and watched the stars swirl over the wine-dark sea as we discussed the lapses and betrayals of the modern world. We should have been helping in the search, but what was the point? Our possessions gone, we felt free in a funny way. We didn't care. We were two whimsical souls colliding in the land of Homer. Half an hour later, the German women came running back, exhilarated and out of breath. "We found everything! Our things! Come!" It was true. Over a sand dune not far away, most of our belongings, including my backpack, were piled together like a happy heap of children hiding in the dark. My backpack had been slashed with a knife and anything of value, like my camera, was gone, but my journal was there and so were most of my clothes, even my toothbrush. It felt like Christmas. I found my sleeping bag and tent in another sand dune and since I hadn't used the tent since Britain anyway, I gave it to Martin because his had been taken. Somehow losing everything and so unexpectedly finding it again had given us a new perspective on what we valued. One of the German women gave me a book. A festive night! The best part of the thievery was that in the semi-crisis of getting our stuff ripped off, I'd met the strange, fair-haired Dutch man and he made me laugh.

Martin and I spent the next two days together talking continuously. Just being with him filled me with an excitement and a calm, deep knowledge. There are people with whom you feel mute and around them you forget you have a head and a heart full of ideas and wonder, poetry and longing, and there are those who can reach straight into your chest and pull songs and stars out of your heart. Martin wasn't quite like that—I didn't sing around him—but he was close, and he was the best friend I'd made in months of traveling. Traveling is so temporary, so peculiar to the nature of the human psyche, that you forget you need friends. When you find one, you remember the miracle of another person and you remember yourself. Talking to Martin made me feel I was availing myself of whatever was extraordinary in the world. He had a special interest in the spirit world, also in plants and modern history. He was a storyteller too, with stories of his long journey through India and Tibet, stories of love, betrayal, auto accidents. I told stories also, most of mine involving medical mishaps in Third World countries.

On the third day Martin left to catch a plane. I walked him to the ferry. He limped because he'd stepped on a sea urchin. He was sunburned. I waved good-bye from the dock to the Dutch man with gawky glasses and violet eyes underneath, and I wondered if I'd ever see him again.

As the days passed, I found it increasingly difficult to leave my wind shelter. I had the moon, sun, stars, my books, the old men in the waves. Why would I leave? I'd seen enough of the world and I liked where I was. Perhaps the more you stay in a place, the more it grows on you, the way some people do. I'd wake at dawn thinking today should be the day to go to another island, go back to the mainland or to another country. But then I'd go for a swim and read a little, take a walk, jump through the waves. The sun would sneak across the sky making its way towards its great dip into the sea and I'd still be there like a lotus eater, lazy some would say, if they didn't know better. One day I decided to take an excursion away from my beach, maybe try to leave it for good. I wasn't prepared to leave Naxos yet. I'd just see more of it. I took a bus to the other side of the island and was gone for four days. It felt like forever.

The bus driver could have gotten us killed several times as he rampaged around hairpin curves into the mountains. From the window, I watched the dramatic patchwork of Naxos, its gardens, vineyards, citrus orchards, villages, and Venetian watchtowers. Farmers plowed with donkeys in the fields. Children played barefoot along the roads. The people of the island may have had only a scruffy flock of goats or a small grape orchard, a rowboat to search the night waters for fish or a *taverna* with three tables, but they weren't poor. Life brought them regular random encounters with friends and relatives each day, not just occasional carefully selected lunches with them. Their lives were rich, plentiful, and cheerful.

I stayed at a fishing village called Apollon on the roof of a house of one of the women in black. In Greece, a woman puts on a black dress when a loved one dies and she wears a black dress the rest of her life. That's devotion. That also cuts down on clothing expenses. Some women also rent out rooms to tourists and, if the rooms are full, they rent the roof. That's a good head for business. By that time I was so accustomed to sleeping outside, I chose the roof over an inside room. The woman in black gave me a fine example of a *tsk tsk*—something people the world over do with their teeth and tongue when they disapprove of you—and she said something in Greek, which was Greek to me, and gave me an extra blanket. For hours I watched the stars and thought of our dark ancestral past far away, the stars where we originated in some distant long forgotten explosion. Under the weight of the stars I could hardly bear the full force of the universe, the randomness, the chaos, the chance of it all. What is one to do with a life when eternity surrounds us?

One could return to a wind shelter under an olive grove. That was one option.

So I returned. And that's when the strange thing happened, the one for which there is no logical explanation. On the first night back from my excursion I had fallen into a deep sleep in my wind shelter when I had the distinct and uncomfortable feeling that something was moving towards me along the beach and I should wake up to chase it away. I tried with all my might to wake up but my eyes felt glued shut and I couldn't open them. The thing was approaching fast, faster every second it seemed, and it was determined, perhaps running, and I knew it was looking for me. Although I couldn't fathom what it was, it felt horribly dangerous and I knew it was imperative I wake up to protect myself. Yet waking was impossible. My body and eyes were paralyzed. Like a great black shadow the thing was coming across the sand and still my body was comatose. Then I could feel it close by and, I knew suddenly, this dark and unknown thing was with me in the olive grove. My heart seemed to bang out of my chest, loud enough to hear. I forced myself to climb up through layers and layers of a deep sleep, the sleep of centuries it felt like, and at last I broke out of it and woke, or so I thought. Pulling myself up on my elbows, I saw what the thing was: a tiny woman in black, no more than four feet tall, and very old. She lay down beside me, curled her body against mine, and shivered. Whatever she was, she was very cold and wanted inside. I knew instinctively she didn't mean inside my sleeping bag. She wanted inside me. No, I said, you can't come in. I live here. She pulled herself closer and her long, damp silver hair fell like sorrow, like misery, like an ancient sad longing. She needed a home, a warm body to live in, a place with a fire. Her face was that of a crone and I could feel her wrinkled icy skin on my cheek. Even her breath was the frigid night air of winter. Her eyes seemed bottomless at first, empty, like black holes, but buried deep inside were two brilliant stars for eyes, blazing stars light years away. Again and again I told her No, which seemed to make her unbearably sad. Please let me in, she pleaded. No, you can't. This is my body, this is me! For a moment an uncanny intimacy hung there between us as we stared at each other across the distance of two worlds. Her eyes shone so brightly they burned my own, burned straight through to my inner core. No, I told her again firmly. No. With that, she was gone. She raised herself up and drifted off down the beach, still shivering and still wanting a home. She left as she had come, with the night breeze.

The incident itself I could easily have dismissed as a weird dream, and did in fact do so the next morning when I woke to the call of the roosters, shaking my head at the previous night's dark madness. Although the dream had been unusually vivid, perceptible and oddly lucid, it had to be a dream nonetheless. A four-foot-tall woman in black trying to pry her way into my body? How rude. Crazy. What happened later that day, however, made me wonder how far dreams travel into the waking world.

That afternoon, the *taverna* near my wind shelter where I always ate lunch was closed, the tables, chairs, and the owner, Nikos, nowhere in sight. Strange, I thought, since I had never seen it closed in all the weeks I'd been there. Perhaps Nikos was taking a holiday. I decided to walk down the beach to the campground restaurant instead. By chance, my table happened to be next to some backpackers who were discussing where they would travel after Greece. As I ate my fruit salad I listened to their conversation, which fortunately was in English since they were of several nationalities. The conversation took a twist when a German woman began to tell the others about a strange dream she'd had the night before.

"It was horrible, a nightmare. I dreamt a little woman came floating along the beach. She was kind of like the women here in Greece, the ones who wear the black, but she was tiny. She was cold. It was terrible, terrible. Such a clear dream."

My spoon fell from my hand and I felt a sudden constriction around my heart. Had I heard her right? Was this too a dream? "Excuse me," I said to the German woman, "I couldn't help overhearing you. What did the woman want?" The German woman looked over at me, startled, almost familiar. Her face was pale.

"To get inside me."

In a land where myth and reality swirl around each other in a luminous haze, lessons clear and absolute can be found after all. I said nothing is murky in Greece but I was wrong. A woman came to me on the mist. She crossed over from the other side and sent me a gift. In all my life I have never known such a moment as when those haunting eyes from eternity stared into mine. Although she may not have intended to, she gave me a message: a human life is an extraordinary treasure. She wanted to feel life, maybe feel it again as she once had, and she wanted it desperately. I was alive, breathing, warm, strong, with a fire and light inside me she ached for. When I pushed her away, proclaiming my life as my own, never had I felt the life inside me so intensely.

I left on the ferry the next day. I didn't need to stay in Naxos anymore. I needed to see the rest of the world. To stay in my wind shelter and live amidst the lure and myth of Greece would be to believe in magic and fate, superstition and dark mysteries. I had this world to explore first, the one with cities and rivers, foreign faces and Woody Allen movies. From the boat I watched the island shrink on the horizon, getting smaller and smaller like a puddle evaporating in the sun.

Yet I knew then as I still know now, that from the shore where the sand dunes begin, the olive grove grows old, and from the bed where we sleep, the shadows of secret things lurk, forbidden, timeless, and forever calling our name.

Laurie Gough's work has appeared in travel literature anthologies, national newspapers and magazines, and Salon.com. This story was excerpted from Kite Strings of the Southern Cross, *which was short-listed for the prestigious Thomas Cook award, and was the silver medal winner of the* ForeWord Magazine *Travel Book of the Year Award. She lives in Ontario, Canada.*

✦ ✦ ✦

Spiritwalker

*On the Big Island, a visiting anthropologist learns
firsthand that Hawai'i's* mana *is real.*

ON THE DAY I FOUND THE *PŌHAKU* [STONE] AWASH IN THE
waves, I had carried it into the old Hawaiian village and placed
it under the tamarind tree just beyond the pond. There it
remained for several months, visited daily by me and the children on our nature walk while I slowly established a relationship with it. I do not know why I did this. I just did.

One day the time seemed right, and I invoked the stone's
spirit in my stone-moving ritual, asking its permission to
bring it away from its beach and to my home. Its strong agree-
ment flowed into me in response. I did not wish to be seen
taking it from the site, so I arrived at the beach early the next
morning before anyone was there and carried the stone to my
car. When I got home, I placed it near my front door in the
rock garden among the other beach stones. There it sat for a
while, untouched. It had made its first voyage, however, from
the wild place of its origin into the world of human beings in
my Volkswagen van.

The curious bond between us continued to develop. The

bond was not merely my thrill at possessing an object for which I felt attraction. The linkage involved a process between myself and the stone. My first hesitant attempts at dialogue were necessarily experimental, but I had an ongoing moment-to-moment awareness of presence. In the beginning I simply let my attention rest upon it meditatively while thoughts and feelings related to it moved through my mind. As the thoughts and feelings took on recurrent patterns, my personal awareness of it deepened.

One night the stone came to me in my dreaming, and upon awakening I saw it in my mind's eye in its completed form. I got up, went out to the stone, and asked its permission to sculpt it. I felt a strong, positive reaction, so that afternoon, I carried it to the tree stump I used as a base for sculpting. With bush hammers, I did a minimum of reducing of the "chin." A little chisel work brought out the "mouth," and it was done. Most of the stone remained untouched, just as I had found it.

I then replaced the *pōhaku* with its attendant sculptures in the rock garden, staring east toward the summit of the volcano of which it was a part. In my thoughts, I addressed it as Kapōhakuki'ihele—the stone that journeys. And as the stone's first custodian—or *kahu*-elect—I too would have ordinary and non-ordinary journeys and discoveries in everyday reality.

Soon after I rendered the stone, I attended a conference held at the Keauhou Beach Hotel, on the coast near Kailua-Kona, an insiders' affair put on by Hawaiians to honor the knowledge and achievements of their Polynesian ancestors. As an outsider, I was fortunate to have been invited——it was the efforts of a curator-photographer friend working at the Kona Historical Society Museum that got me an invitation. The conference was well attended by an interesting gathering of people, most of whom were of Polynesian descent. Professor Rubellite Kawena Johnson of the University of Hawai'i spoke about the *heiau* and about the Hawaiian gods and ceremonies. Hawaiian elders Papa Kala Nali'i'elua and David Mauna Roy spoke about the traditional Hawaiian world view and the intimate connection between Hawaiian culture and the land. They described the Hawaiians' respect for nature and how the Polynesians had taken care of the land, seeking harmony with it so that it would take care of them. They spoke of the Hawaiian concept of spiritual unity with their *'aumakua*, their ancestral spirits, and how life and *mana* (supernatural or divine power) came out of everything in nature.

Another session was held by four crew members of the now-famous double-hulled voyaging canoe *Hōkūle'a*. This sixty-foot re-creation of a traditional Hawaiian transoceanic sailing vessel has completed many round trips between Hawai'i and Tahiti, as well as a long voyage to New Zealand and back. The *haku* of the canoe, Captain Shorty Bertelmann, was there, as was the watch captain, Tava Taupu. Sam Ka'ai spoke strongly about the place of the sailing canoe in traditional Hawaiian society and revealed that the ancient Order of the Canoe was being reformed to "refill the bowl with what had been lost."

A trim, handsome young man of Hawaiian descent was introduced. His name was Nainoa Thompson, the first Hawaiian in more than six centuries to navigate a great sailing canoe over the vast oceanic expanses of Polynesia without modern-day instruments. The respect and the awe in which this man is held is great. As navigator of the canoe, he is the most important crew member, the one into whose care the success of the voyage and the lives of all the voyagers are entrusted. He is the wayfinder. I had never heard of him before that moment.

Partially trained by a traditional Micronesian navigator named Mau Piailug, Nainoa Thompson rediscovered the ancient Polynesian navigational system that used the stars, moon, clouds, winds, ocean swells, and currents. He re-created the way-finding method that had brought his ancestors to Hawai'i in several waves of migration, beginning around A.D. 300.

Nainoa Thompson spoke in a soft voice about his voyages and his ancestors and about harmony. He spoke with integrity, with power, and with humility—and he never mentioned himself. He talked about the canoe and the crew, the ocean and the heavens. All of these became one, he said, balanced and unified during the voyage. He suggested that this unity was the goal and the success of the journey—a goal in which each person was as important as everyone else.

The Hawaiians in the audience were misty-eyed with pride of him and, through him, for themselves. The *mana* generated by their collective emotion was palpable in the room.

After his talk I waited for an opportunity to approach him. We shook hands and exchanged pleasantries. I wondered what moved through his mind and through his dreaming as he guided the double-hulled canoe across the vast expanses of the watery world. I wondered what it would be like to be out there with him. What would my own dreams produce under those circumstances?

The last session at the conference was conducted by a Hawaiian healer, a *kahuna lapa'au* named Morrnah Nalamaku Simeona, who shared her knowledge and skill in *ho'opono'ono*, the traditional Hawaiian method of conflict resolution.

She spoke of the unity and balance of life and how everything in life begins with thought and intention. She discussed the three levels of being—the physical, the mental, and the spiritual—as they are conceived within traditional Hawaiian spiritual knowledge. She spoke of how these three aspects are manifested within human beings: the spiritual as the super-conscious mind or *'aumakua*, the mental as the conscious mind or *'uhane*, the physical as a material form, the body, and a non-material form, the subconscious mind or *'unihipili*.

These concepts are not unique to Hawaiian culture and are well known to Western psychology, but hearing Morrnah Simeona's talk made me want to know more about Hawaiian shamanism and the body of knowledge called Ho'omana, or Hawaiian mysticism.

After her talk I politely asked her to clarify a point she had made about healing. She gave me a curious look and then reached out, took my hand in both of hers and closed her eyes. Long moments passed. Then she smiled and looked at me again, her alert gaze boring into mine and asked me if I knew what *aloha* really meant. "It means to be in the presence of the divinity," she explained. "*Alo* means 'to be in the presence of' and *ha* is 'the divine breath of life'—*alo-haaa*." She paused as if to see the effect of her words.

"Problems always begin in the mind, in the mental aspect," she continued. "Physical and psychological problems have their source in negative thought-forms. Illness is an effect of these distorted thoughts. Unfavorable thoughts arise in the conscious mind and are then held in the subconscious from which they can be transferred into the physical body. Because of this, true healing always has to begin at the spiritual level.

"One must ask the divinity for help. Then the divinity sends down its *ha* through one's *'aumakua* level of self. From one's spiritual aspect, it travels into the subconscious level of the physical. This deep level of the mind can then erase the negative thought-forms and emotions it holds, such as anger and fear, replacing them with light. This is how the cause of illness is dealt with and how all true healing is accomplished."

She smiled again and released my hand. Someone else

asked her a question, but for long moments her gaze remained locked with mine as she looked into my soul. I do not know what she saw there, but she nodded slightly and beamed warmly at me before turning away.

I remained rooted to the spot while the crowd surged around me like water around a rock. I felt something within my body—something that had flowed from her to me during those brief moments. I recognized it as the sensation of power. I realized that I had received *mana* from her, transmitted through her touch. I felt something deep within me open in response. The sensation remained there, just below the surface, throughout the rest of the day.

This experience marked the beginning of my investigation into Ho'omana.

Hank Wesselman is a professional anthropologist who taught courses in anthropology for the University of California at San Diego and the University of Hawai'i at Hilo. He and his family divide their time between Northern California, where he teaches anthropology at American College and Sierra College, and Hawai'i, where they own and work a small farm. This piece was excerpted from his book, Spiritwalker: Messages from the Future.

✷ ✷ ✷

Under the Brush Arbor

God takes strange forms in Alabama.

THE CARD HE PRESSED INTO MY HAND READ: "CHARLES McGlocklin, the End-Time Evangelist." "You can have as much of God as you want," he said. His voice was low and urgent. "These seminary preachers don't understand that. They don't understand the spirit of the Lord. They're taught by man. They know the forms of godliness, but they deny the power."

Brother Charles was a big man in his early fifties with a full head of dark hair and hands the size of waffle irons. He didn't have a church himself, and he didn't particularly want one. He'd preached on the radio, he said, and at county fairs and trade days. In years past, he'd driven all over the South, conducting revivals under a tent he'd hauled in the back of his '72 Chevy van. He said he had even stood on the road in front of his house trailer in New Hope, Alabama, and preached at passing cars.

"I get a lot of stares," he added, and then he put his big hand on my shoulder and drew me toward him confidentially.

"I have received visitations by angels," he said. "One of them was seven feet tall. It was a frightening experience."

I said I bet it was.

"And I'll tell you something else," he said. "One night I was fasting and praying on the mountain, and I was taken out in the spirit. The Lord appeared to me in layers of light." His grip tightened on my shoulder. "He spoke a twelve-hour message to me on one word: polluted."

"Polluted?"

"Yes. Polluted. Now, you think about that for a minute. A twelve-hour message."

I thought about it for a minute, and then decided Brother Charles was out of his mind.

In time, I'd find out he wasn't, despite the fact that he kept four copperheads in a terrarium on his kitchen counter between the Mr. Coffee and the microwave. He said God moved on him one night to handle a big timber rattler right there in the kitchen. His wife, Aline, showed me a photo of him doing it. Aline was thirteen years younger than Charles, childlike and frankly beautiful, a Holiness mystic from Race Track Road who worked the night shift weaving bandage gauze. "I had just got up, getting ready to go to work," she said, "and my camera was just laying there." She pointed at the photo. "You see how the Holy Ghost moved on him?"

In the photo, Charles is standing in the kitchen in his white t-shirt and jeans. He has a rattlesnake in one hand, and he appears to be shouting at it as though it were a sensible and rebellious thing. "There's serpents, and then there's fiery serpents," Charles said. "That one was a fiery serpent."

Another time, Charles said he wanted to take up a serpent real bad, but he didn't have one on hand. The Holy Ghost told him, "You don't have a snake, but you've got a heater." So Charles ran to the wood-burning stove in the living room and laid his hands on it. "Baby, that thing was hot," he said. But his hands, when he finally took them off the stove, weren't a bit burned. Instead, they were as cold as a block of ice, he said.

Aline reminded him that he did get a blister from a skillet once, but Charles said, "God wasn't in that. That was in myself. That's why I got burned."

"You were just thinking about that corn bread," Aline added with a knowing smile.

Long before I was a guest in their home, I'd seen the McGlocklins at services at The Church of Jesus with Signs Following in Scottsboro. We became friends, and then something more than friends, but that is a long and complicated story that began, I think, on the afternoon of my first brush arbor meeting on top of Sand Mountain, when Aline was taken out in the spirit, and I accompanied her on tambourine.

I had never even heard of a brush arbor until J. L. Dyal built one in a field behind his house near the Sand Mountain town of Section in the summer of 1992. Brother Carl had invited me to the services, and J.L. had drawn a map. "You take a left at the Sand Mountain Dragway sign," he said. "We'll get started just before sundown."

I was pleased the handlers had felt comfortable enough to include me. It meant the work was going well. The relationship between journalist and subject is often an unspoken conspiracy. The handlers wanted to show me something, and I was ready to be shown. It seemed to me that the [attempted murder] conviction of Glenn Summerford was not the end of their story, but simply the beginning of another chapter. I was interested in what would happen to them now that Glenn was in prison and The Church of Jesus with Signs Following had split. But I had a personal agenda too. I was enjoying the passion and abandon of their worship. Vicki didn't seem to mind. She encouraged me to go. So I told Brother Carl and J.L. I'd be there for the brush arbor services, although I couldn't visualize what they were talking about. "Brush arbor" seemed a contradictory term. The word arbor suggested civilized restraint. The word brush didn't.

I did know that outdoor revivals had once been commonplace in the rural South. The most famous occurred in 1801, when thousands of renegade Presbyterians, in their rebellion against stiff-necked Calvinism, gathered in a field near Cane Ridge, Kentucky, for a week-long camp meeting. They were soon joined by Methodists and Baptists, until their combined ranks swelled to more than 25,000, a crowd many times greater than the population of the largest town in Kentucky at the time. Something inexplicable and portentous happened to many of the worshipers in that field near Cane Ridge. Overcome by the Holy Spirit, they began to shriek, bark, and jerk. Some fell to the ground as though struck dead. "Though so awful to behold," wrote one witness, "I do not remember that any one of the thousands...ever sustained an injury in body."

Cane Ridge set the stage for the dramatic events at a mission on Azusa Street in Los Angeles in 1906, when the Holy Ghost descended in power on a multiracial congregation led by a one-eyed black preacher named William Seymour, and the great American spiritual phenomenon of the twentieth century, Pentecostalism, began in a fury of tongue speaking and prophesying and healing.

Cane Ridge had been the prototype of revivalism on a grand scale. The crowd at J.L.'s brush arbor was somewhat smaller—thirteen of us altogether, plus a gaggle of curious on-lookers who hid behind Brother Carl Porter's Dodge Dakota pickup. But the facilities at J.L.'s were top-notch. Traditional brush arbors had been small and temporary, primitive shelters usually built at harvest time from whatever materials might be at hand. Willow branches were especially prized because of their flexibility. Thick vines added strength. The idea was to give field hands a place to worship so they wouldn't have to leave the premises before all the crops were in. But J.L. had constructed his brush arbor out of sturdy two–by–fours over which he had stretched sheets of clear plastic so that services could be held even in a downpour. The vines and brush piled on top of the plastic appeared to be decorative rather than functional, yielding the impression of a brush arbor without all its inconveniences. J.L.'s father-in-law, Dozier Edmonds, had helped string electricity to the structure and had installed a length of track lighting. The place was perfect, except for one thing. There weren't any snakes.

"I thought you were going to bring them," said Brother Carl to Brother Charles.

"I thought Brother Willie was going to bring them," Charles replied. He was getting his guitar out of the car, an in-strument the Lord, he said, had taught him to play.

"Brother Willie got serpent bit last night," Carl reminded him.

"I know, but he said he was going to be here today."

"Maybe I need to check on him after the service," Carl said. "It was a copperhead," he confided to me. "Over in Georgia. Bit him on the thumb, but it didn't hurt him bad."

"Well, we don't have to have serpents to worship the Lord," Charles finally said. He put his boot up on a pine bench that would serve as the altar and began strumming the guitar. When everyone had gathered around, he started to sing. "He's God in Alabama. He's God in Tennessee. He's God in North Carolina. He's God all over me. Oh, God is God…and Jesus is his name…"

The service had begun at five o'clock to avoid the midafternoon heat. The light was low and golden over the

field, and Charles's voice rose above it like a vapor, unampli-
fied, snatched away by the breeze. Aline was there; Brother
Carl and the old prophetess, Aunt Daisy; J.L. and his wife,
Dorothea; one of their daughters-in-law and her baby; and
Dorothea's father, Dozier, and her mother, Burma, who had a
twin sister named Erma. Both Burma and Erma, 68, attended
snake-handling services, usually in identical dresses, but only
Burma actually handled.

I'd also brought photographers Jim Neel and Melissa
Springer with me, and they moved quietly around the edges
of the arbor as the service picked up steam. The choice of
photographers had been simple. Jim was one of my oldest
friends. In addition to being a sculptor and painter, he'd
worked with me as a combat photographer in Central
America during the 1980s. Melissa, whose work I'd first noticed when it was censored by police at an outdoor exhibit in
Birmingham, had been documenting the lives of men and
women clinging to the underbelly of the American dream—
female impersonators, dancers with AIDS, women inmates in
the HIV isolation unit at Alabama's Julia Tutwiler prison.
When I told her about the snake handlers, she said she had to
meet them, but unlike most people who say they want to, she
kept calling and insisting that we set a time. She and Jim were
an interesting study in contrasts: he was moody, private, and
intense; Melissa was warm, expansive, and maternal. But both
were obsessed with their work, easy to travel with, and open
to possibilities.

Melissa had worn an ankle-length dress this time. At her
first service in Scottsboro, she'd gotten the message when
Aunt Daisy prophesied against the wearing of pants by
women. Outsiders are bound to get preached at a little in
Holiness churches. But the same Holiness preachers who draw

attention to unorthodox details of behavior or dress inevitably hugged us after the service and invited us back.

Some preachers didn't take the Holiness prescriptions about dress quite as seriously as others. Charles McGlocklin's theory was simple: "You've got to catch the fish before you clean them." His wife, Aline, didn't wear makeup or cut her hair, but she occasionally allowed herself the luxury of a brightly colored hair ornament. "God looks at the heart, anyway. He doesn't look on the outside," she said. She also drove a white Chevy Beretta with an airbrushed tag that read "Aline loves Charles." Charles's pickup had a matching tag, with "Charles loves Aline." Both sentiments were inscribed in the middle of interlocking hearts, like the brightly colored hearts on Aline's hair clasp.

Despite the empty chairs and the lack of electric guitars or serpents, the worship at J.L.'s brush arbor followed the same pattern I'd experienced in Scottsboro. Without church walls, it seemed more delicate and temporal, though, and Brother Carl's sermon echoed the theme. He talked about the flesh as grass, passing in a moment, of earthly life being short and illusory. He talked about the body as "fleshy rags" that he would gladly give up in exchange for a heavenly wardrobe. But at the center of Carl's sermon was the topic of God's love, which he seemed to first discover fully even as he talked his way into it.

"It's got no end," he said, "no bottom, no ceiling. Paul says nothing can separate us from the love of God through Jesus Christ. And let me tell you, sometimes we find His love in the little things. The fact that we're here today is a sign God loves us." Amen. "The fact that we got a brain to think with, and a tongue to speak with, and a song to sing. I just want to thank Him for waking me up this morning," he said. "I want to thank Him for giving me food to eat and a roof over my head. Sometimes we ask Him to work big miracles, but forget to thank Him for the little ones." Amen. "But he's a great big God, and He never fails. His grace is sufficient to meet our every need. He's a good God, isn't He?" And everybody said amen.

Then Carl invited Brother Charles to give his testimony. In Holiness churches, a testimony is a personal story that reveals God's power and grace. It's not meant to exhort or instruct the congregation—that would be preaching—but simply to praise the Lord. In practice, though, the line between testifying and preaching is not so clear-cut.

Brother Carl and Brother Charles hugged, and after a few introductory comments about the beauty of the afternoon and the love he felt from everybody gathered there, Brother Charles began to testify. It was a story, both lurid and familiar, that could only have come from the South.

"Up until I was five years old," Charles said, "I lived in a tent on the banks of the Tennessee River at Old Whitesburg Bridge. Y'all know where that's at. Then my mother got remarried, and we moved to a houseboat at Clouds Cove."

Clouds Cove.

"My stepdaddy was drunk."

"Amen," said J.L., who knew something about drunks himself.

"My real daddy lived to be eighty," Charles said. "He died in the Tennessee penitentiary, where he was serving a life sentence for killing his second wife. I was like a lamb thrown into a den of lions when we moved to Clouds Cove," Charles said. "In 1948, when I was six, we lived on nothing but parched corn for three weeks, like rats. We slept on grass beds. We didn't even have a pinch of salt. Now, that's poor."

Amen. They all knew what it was like to be poor.

"By the time I was eight, I'd seen two men killed in our house. I was afraid to go to sleep at night."

Help him, Jesus.

"I made it to the eighth grade, but when I was just shy of turning thirteen years old, I got shot in the stomach with a twelve-gauge shotgun. That was the first time I heard the audible voice of God."

Praise His holy name!

"There I was, holding my insides in my hands. Then things, they really colored up funny, I thought to myself. Then I had the awfullest fear come up on me," Charles said. He was pacing back and forth by now, a loping, methodical pace, his huge, dog-eared Bible held loosely in one hand like an implement. "I saw a vision of my casket lid closing on me, and the voice out of heaven spoke to me and said, 'Don't be afraid, cause everything's gonna be all right,' and I felt that shield of faith just come down on me!"

Hallelujah!

"God's been good to me!"

Amen.

"He's been good to me!"

Amen.

"Doctors told my mother I had maybe fifteen minutes to live. 'There's no way he can make it,' they said. 'Almost all his liver's shot out, almost all his stomach.' I was on the operating table sixteen to eighteen hours. They had to take out several yards of intestines. I stayed real bad for forty-two days and nights. I was one hundred twenty pounds when I got shot and eighty-seven when I got out of that hospital. But just look at me now!"

Praise His name!

Brother Charles was standing with his hands clenched at his side and a wild look in his eyes. He was a big man, an enormous man. It was not the first time I'd noticed that, but it was the first time I had considered the damage he might do if he ever had a reason.

"God's been good to me!" he said as he started pacing again.

Amen.

"I said He's been good to me!"

Amen!

He suddenly stopped in his tracks. "But I wasn't always good to Him."

"Now you're telling it," Brother Carl said.

"When I was sixteen, I went to live with my real daddy in Tennessee," Charles said. "He was one of the biggest moonshiners in the state, and I wanted to learn the trade. I dabbled in it a good long time. I was bad. I went up to Chicago and did some other things I shouldn't have."

Tell it. They'd all done things they shouldn't have.

"When I came back South, I drove a long-haul rig twice a week to New York City. Then I bought me a thirty-three acre farm in Minor Hill, Tennessee. Two-story house. Fine car. I had a still upstairs that could run forty to fifty gallons of whiskey, and in another room I stored my bales of marijuana. Pretty good for a boy who'd grown up picking cotton."

Amen. They knew about cotton.

He raised his Bible and shook it at us. "I don't have to tell you that's the deceitfulness of riches talking, boys."

Preach on.

"One day, things had really got bad on me. I had just got under so much that I couldn't go no further, and I was getting ready to kill myself. The devil spoke to me and said, 'Just go ahead and take that gun and kill yourself and get it over with.'"

No, Lord.

He walked to the edge of the arbor and pantomimed picking something up from the grass. "I went over there and got the gun and was fixing to put a shell in it, and when I did, this other voice came to me and said, 'Put that gun back down and walk back over in front of that wood heater.'"

Amen.

"I walked back over there in front of the wood heater, and suddenly that power from on high hit me in the head and knocked me down on my knees, and I said six words. I won't never forget what they was. I said, 'Lord, have mercy on my soul.'"

Amen. Thank God.

"He took me out in the spirit and I came back speaking in other tongues as the Spirit gave utterance. The devil said, 'Look, look now. Now what are you going to do?' He said, 'Look at all that moonshine, all that marijuana you got. What are you going to do now? Ain't you in a mess now? Here you are, you've got the Holy Ghost, and you've got all this in your house.' And the Lord spoke to me and said, 'Just set your house in order.'"

Bless him, Lord!

"He said, 'Just set your house in order!'"

Amen!

"So that's what I did. I set my house in order. I got rid of that moonshine and marijuana. I told the devil to depart that place in the name of Jesus, and within a year I'd taken up my first serpent."

Amen.

"We've got to set our house in order!" Charles said, and now he was leaning toward us, red-faced, with flecks of white spittle in the corners of his mouth. "We're in the last days with the Lord, children! He won't strive with man forever! He's a merciful God, he's a loving God, but you better believe he's also a just God, and there will come a time when we'll have to account for these lives we've led! We better put our house in order!"

Amen. Thank God. Bless the sweet name of Jesus.

There were only thirteen people under that brush arbor, but it seemed like there were suddenly three hundred. They were jumping and shouting, and pretty soon Brother Carl was anointing Burma and Erma with oil, and Brother Charles had launched into "Jesus on My Mind" on his guitar, and J.L. and I had our tambourines going. There was so much racket that at first it was hard to hear what Aline was doing over in the corner by a length of dog wire that the morning glory vines had twined around. Her back was to us. Her hands were in the air, and she was rocking slowly from side to side, her face upturned and her voice quavering, *"Akiii, akiii, akiii. Akiii, akiii, akiii…"*

It was the strangest sound I had ever heard. At first, it did not seem human. It sounded like the voice of a rare night bird, or some tiny feral mammal. And then the voice got louder, mounting up on itself, until it started to sound like that of a child who was lost and in great pain. But even as the hairs on my arm started to stand on end, the voice turned into something else, a sound that had pleasure in it as well as torment. Ecstasy, I would learn later, is excruciating, but I did not know that then.

"Akiii, akiii, akiii…" The singing and praising elsewhere in the brush arbor had started to diminish. Brother Charles had stopped strumming his guitar. Brother Carl had put away his oil. Burma and Dorothea kept their hands raised, but except for an occasional amen or praise Jesus, the air fell silent around Aline's voice. Everyone was listening to her now. I could not disentangle myself from the sound of her voice, the same syllables repeated with endless variation. At times, it seemed

something barbed was being pulled from her throat; at other times, the sound was a clear stream flowing outward into thin air. Her voice seemed to be right in my ear. It was a sobbing. A panting after something she could not quite reach. And then it would be a coming to rest in some exquisite space, a place so tender it could not be touched without *"Akiii, akiii, akiii…"* The sun had set and the electric lights were not yet turned on, but the arbor seemed filled with a golden light. We were swaying in it, transfixed, with Aline silhouetted against the dog wire and the morning glory vines. All but her trembling voice was silent, or so it seemed, until I realized with horror that my tambourine was still going, vibrating against my leg, almost apart from me, as if it had a motive and direction of its own.

My hand froze. It was as though I had been caught in some act of indecency. But Aline's voice reacted with renewed desperation, *"Akiii, akiii, akiii,"* and so I let the tambourine have its own way, now louder and faster, until it almost burst into a song, and then softer and more slowly, until it resembled the buzzing of a rattlesnake in a serpent box. It anticipated every move that Aline's voice made, and vice versa. The intimacy was unnerving: her voice and the tambourine, perfectly attuned to one another and moving toward the same end. I was unreasonably afraid that Charles would be angry with me. I didn't yet know the full dimensions of passion. It was much later that I would come to understand what had gone on in that moment. The tambourine was simply accompanying Aline while she felt for and found God. And I mean "accompany" in its truest sense: "to occur with." And nobody could predict when something like that might happen. Through the tambourine, I was occurring with her in the Spirit, and it was not of my own will.

I cannot say how long the episode lasted. It seemed to go

on for a very long time. J.L. turned the lights on at the end.
The men hugged the men. The women hugged the women.
Aline and I shook hands. If the snake handlers found anything
unusual about our curious duet afterward, they never spoke
directly to me about it. But I do know one thing: it was after
that brush arbor meeting on Sand Mountain that they started
to call me Brother Dennis.

*Dennis Covington teaches creative writing at the University of
Alabama at Birmingham. He writes on the South for* The New
York Times *and is the author of the award-winning novel* Lizard
and Salvation on Sand Mountain: Snake Handling and
Redemption in Southern Appalachia, *from which this story was
excerpted. He lives in Birmingham with his wife, novelist Vicki
Covington, and their two daughters.*

DONALD W. GEORGE

* * *

In Notre Dame

*Visiting a Parisian landmark, the author
is moved by the Unseen.*

NOTRE DAME FROM THE OUTSIDE IS MAGNIFICENT, MONU-
mental, solidly of the earth and yet soaringly not. But for all
its monumental permanence, its context is clearly the present:
visitors pose, focus, click; portable stalls sell sandwiches and
postcards; tourist groups shuffle by in ragtag formation.

Walk through those massive, humbling doors, though, and
suddenly you breathe the air of antiquity. Let your mind and
eyes adjust to the inner light, and you begin to realize that there
is much more to Paris than the life of its streets, and a small
sense of its magnificent and moving past comes back to you.

When I entered Notre Dame on my most recent trip, I was
overwhelmed by the solid, soaring arches and columns I had
forgotten, by the depth and texture of the stained-glass windows with their luminous blues and reds and greens. I thought
of how many people had worked to build this magnificence,
and of how many people since then had stood, perhaps on the
very same stones as I, and marveled at it. I thought of all the
faith and hope and sacrifice it manifests. I walked through the

fervent space, awed by the art and the hush that seemed to resonate with the whispers of centuries, and just when I was beginning to feel too small and insignificant and was getting ready to leave, I saw a simple sign over a tiny stone basin of water, on a column near the doors.

The sign said, "In the name of the Father and the Son and the Holy Spirit" in seven languages, with pictures that showed a hand dipping into the water, then touching a forehead.

I touched my hand to the cool, still water, then brought it to my head, and as I did so, chills ran through my body and tears streamed into my eyes.

Somehow that simple act had forged a palpable contact with ages past, had put everything into startling focus: the ceaseless flow of pilgrims to this special place, the ceaseless procession of hands to water and fingers to forehead, all sharing this basin, this gesture.

I felt a new sense of the history that flows with us and around us and beyond us all—of the plodding, tireless path of humankind and of the sluggish, often violent spread of Christianity through Europe and the rest of the world—and a new sense of the flow of my own history, too: my Protestant upbringing, a pastor whose notions of Christian love have had a deep and abiding influence on my life, the old and still inconceivable idea of God.

For a few moments I lost all sense of place and time—then a door opened and a tourist group entered, looking up and around in wonder, and I walked into the world of sunlight and spire again.

I stopped, blinked at the sandwich stalls and postcard vendors, then turned back toward that stony symmetry and thought: sometimes you feel so small and insignificant in the crush of history that you lose all sense of purpose and self. Then something will happen to make you realize that every act and every encounter has its own precious meaning and lesson, and that history is simply the sum of all these.

Sometimes it comes together, as it did for me that moment in Notre Dame; sometimes the world is reduced to a simple sign, a stone basin, the touch of water to head—and the vast pageant of the past and the living parade of the present take on a new, and renewing, symmetry and sense.

For eight years Donald W. George was the award-winning travel editor of the San Francisco Examiner. *His career as a peripatetic scribbler started in Paris, where he lived and worked and fell in love (several times) the summer between his junior and senior years at Princeton. He is the co-editor of* Travelers' Tales Japan, *and now works for Lonely Planet Publications. He lives with his family in Oakland, California.*

JAMES G. COWAN

✦ ✦ ✦

Rai

In Australia, the author visits an ancient place,
and encounters ancient knowledge.

"YOU'RE IN LUCK TODAY," THE LIBRARIAN REMARKED, PEER-
ing through the doorway into the wide, sunlit street beyond.
"There's Mr. Rouse now. I see his vehicle pulling up outside."
Harvey Rouse was a small, wiry sort of man who I judged to
be in his late seventies, possibly older. Wearing a bush hat that
had been pushed out of shape years ago, he walked in a hurried manner that belied his age. He came toward us along the
path, his shirt buttoned almost to the neck, his knobby knees
protruding from a pair of faded khaki shorts. He reminded me
of a gremlin or a garden gnome. It was hard to believe that he
had spent most of his life working among Aborigines in some
of the most remote places in the world. His mannerisms were
most like those of a staff sergeant or hospital orderly than
those of a scholar.

The librarian introduced me to the explorer, and we shook
hands. Knowing that Mr. Rouse was the first European since
George Grey to step inside a Wandjina cave made him, in my
eyes at least, someone special. As an old bushman who had

spent many years of his life sitting around campfires learning the Natingin language from the last of the Aboriginal elders, he was in a category all his own. I was keen to know to what extent they had shared their secrets with him.

"Why don't you come to dinner this evening and we can talk," Mr. Rouse said, generously extending the invitation when I explained the reason for my visit to Derby. He agreed to pick me up in his aging Toyota outside the hostel at around six o'clock.

Later that evening Mr. Rouse drove me to his place on the outskirts of town. I soon found myself gazing at the high wire gate guarding the entry to an earth-moving machinery site deep in the scrub. There were no lights in the place. Mr. Rouse unlocked the chain on the gate, then drove his vehicle past the shadowy bulk of front-end loaders toward a group of buildings in the far corner. The atmosphere in the yard was like that of a Roman ruin at night. I felt somewhat uncomfortable, especially when I learned that Mr. Rouse had been forced to live out his twilight years in three old workman's huts that he had managed to scrounge from the Department of Main Roads.

"They travel everywhere with me," Mr. Rouse remarked with some pride. "The owner of the worksite offered me the land in return for caretaking duties when I retired. So I brought my huts over here from where I was living. You must think me a regular tortoise, carrying my house around like this!"

"You don't want to live in town?"

"I like the silence out here at night. Derby is too noisy for me. This place keeps me in touch with the bush."

Inside the first hut I was introduced to a world of cobwebs, large mosquitoes, a small table cluttered with food, a bed piled high with clothing, and a fridge. The bulb above our heads threw down a vague light, nothing more. A much-thumbed copy of the Bible lay by the window among assorted manuscripts and old newspapers. I immediately realized that "dinner" was likely to be a couple of cheese sandwiches washed down with a mug of tea. Old bushmen rarely linger over food; tinned beef and damper (bread made in a camp oven from flour mixed with water) form their staple diet when they're on the move.

"Tell me about the time when you found Grey's cave," I began as Mr. Rouse extracted a slab of cheese from a packet.

"During the war, it was," he replied. "I had been working on a mission in east Naringin country for a number of years. An anthropologist friend of mine in Sydney asked me if I might like to look for Grey's cave on his behalf. It was too far for him to come over here, and anyway nobody traveled in those days because of gasoline restrictions. Of course I jumped at the chance. I always wanted to rediscover those lost Wandjina paintings. But I needed a couple of good boys to help me find the cave. In the end I asked the administrator at the mission if he would give me my pick."

Mr. Rouse laughed at the memory.

"He agreed, but on the condition that I cut wood for him for three weeks. That's how I came by my Aboriginal guides. In the end they cost me a load of wood!"

"And a few blisters, I'll bet," I said. "Did they lead you straight to the cave?"

"Not at all. I had only a hand-traced map my friend had sent me. Trying to decipher this was no easy matter. We spent weeks wandering about the country hoping to find what we were looking for. Real rubbish country it was, too. The donkeys were a godsend, though. Horses would never have been able to cross that terrain. Too rough."

"You found the cave in the end, though."

"Yeah. But I tell you it was a spooky place to come upon. In all my life I've never felt so strange entering a cave. The Wandjinas on the wall were like figures from outer space. Here I was, in the presence of a group of beings looking down at me, almost as if they were interrogating me with their gaze. They had huge eyes and no mouths. I felt as if I had stumbled into a sort of living hell, like you see on church walls in Europe sometimes."

"Can you recall what color the figures were?"

"White, mostly. With black eyes surrounded by orange, ocher-colored circles. Their noses were the same color. But what made them appear really odd was a thick orange nimbus, like a horseshoe, with rays radiating from above their heads."

"Like the ray on the signboard of a public house," I said, recalling Grey's description.

"That's about right," Mr. Rouse agreed.

"Did they have bodies?"

"Sort of, but all that wasn't very clear. They looked vaguely like ghosts, I suppose. The painting was in pretty poor shape, you must understand. The old fellas hadn't been up there to repaint them in years."

"The Aboriginal elders, you mean?"

"Yeah. In the old days, when the tradition was strong, they used to visit the cave each year before the wet season to perform rituals and repaint the Wandjina. According to Woolagoodja, one of my guides, they prayed to them when they wanted rain. That was their way of bringing on the wet season. He was good man, old Woolly. He knew his stuff really well."

"Perhaps there's someone else in Derby you might recommend I talk to about the Wandjina," I said.

"Well, there's my principal informant on the Naringin language," he suggested. "His name is Waljali. He's what they call a sites officer here in town. Between him and his friend, old Kamurro, I reckon they know about all there is to know on the Wandjina these days. Most of the old blokes have died, you see. And the young ones know nothing. All they're interested in is grog and women, nothing more. Kamurro happens to be a sorcerer, which makes him rather special. He knows a lot about the old ways."

"He's a medicine man?"

"They call them *barnmunji* around here. I wrote a paper on them once. Hold on, let me see if I can find it for you."

Mr. Rouse went to a cabinet by the wall next to his bed and rummaged in one of the drawers. He produced a sheaf of papers at last and handed them to me. The title of the article was "The *Rai* and the Inner Eye."

"You can have it," he said. "I've got no use for it anymore. It could prove interesting to you if you want to know more about Aboriginal ways. Don't know why, though," he added dismissively.

Flipping quickly through the pages, I came across a Naringin text with an English translation written underneath. A few words caught my interest at once: *Wandjina djiri: ru; dambun djuman mana, yadmerinanganari.* Underneath was transcribed: "*Wandjina* is the important one. We say concerning him that he designed the world."

Later, when Mr. Rouse had dropped me back at the hostel, I wasted no time in beginning his article on the *rai*. It was a remarkable document, unlike any I had come across before on the subject. Not only did it describe the creation of the world to the Wandjina, but it also detailed the making of a *barnmunji* with the help of spirit beings known as the *rai*. It seemed that these *rai* had the power to transform a man into someone capable of seeing through the veil of ordinary reality with the aid of a so-called inner eye—that is, a quality of spiritual perception not available to the conventional run of men.

According to the document, the *rai* are spirit children who live in the bush and wander about at night. Men can encounter them only in their dreams. Furthermore, a *rai* is a sort of "spirit double" of the man, and is therefore capable of telling him how his country is faring when the man happens to be absent from it for some reason. According to the text, the *rai* feeds on its own arm blood and is therefore self-sustaining. The *rai's* main task is to give a *barnmunji* the power of visionary perception so that he can see with his inner eye, aided by the use of *gedji* or quartz crystals. These are pressed into the *barnmunji's* body in a magical fashion. But once the crystals are lodged in his body, he is equipped with supernatural powers that enable him to attend to the sick, perform new *corroborees* (sacred dances), and travel great distances through the air.

My first impression after reading about the *rai* was to ask myself whether Mr. Rouse had deliberately set out to mislead me. The concept of the *rai* seemed so preposterous that I began to wonder whether the old man had been affected by the sun. Spirit doubles, inserting quartz crystals into the body, vampirelike creatures that fed on their own arm blood, astral travel—these descriptions seemed to draw their inspiration from the shadowy realm of the occult rather than from any bona fide religious experience. Then I recalled the first words of the text: "Wandjini is the important one. He made the world." Such an emphatic statement made me reconsider my initial doubts. I decided to suspend my judgment, at least until after I had discussed these matters with the Aboriginal elders Mr. Rouse had referred me to.

The Mowanjum Aboriginal community outside Derby was

my first stop. Mr. Rouse had advised me to go there and meet with Waljali and Kamurro. He did point out, however, that these men often paid visits to their tribal country, and so might not be at home. Such was the nature of Aboriginal life today, where many tribes find it impossible to live in the bush now that much of their land belonged to pastoralists. The community had been founded for displaced Aborigines who wanted a secure place to bring up their children and be near to medical facilities. The word *mowanjum* meant "settled" or "on firm ground."

I bicycled out to the settlement early one morning. A collection of galvanized-iron shelters and abandoned motor vehicles met my gaze as I rode through the gate. People wandered aimlessly from one shelter to another as they attempted to put some order into an otherwise unvarying day. Hunting and food gathering activities had given way to weekly government pension checks for most of these tribespeople as they struggled to come to terms with their state of exile. I felt a certain sadness watching children roll bicycle rims across a clearing, knowing that in the old days they would have been out in the bush with their kinsmen learning how to hunt.

One of these children soon led me to an encampment lying in the shade of some trees. A number of women were sitting on the ground, their dogs asleep nearby. When I approached and asked where I might find Waljali or Kamuro, they fell silent. They looked at me as if I were only half there. It was the look all oppressed people offer to those whom they believe to be responsible for their plight.

Eventually an older woman in the group pointed rather diffidently to my right. I noticed a solitary figure sitting cross-legged under a tree, his head bent over some object in his lap. At no time did the woman speak. I thanked the ladies and made my way over to the man. He stopped whatever he was doing to observe my approach.

"Are you Waljali, or Kamurro?" I asked.

I estimated the man to be in his late sixties. His features were slender, rather refined in appearance. A loosely clipped beard covered his jaw, and his graying hair was swept back from his forehead to reveal partial baldness. His eyes appraised me as if I were standing some distance away. Though I had approached him in the spirit of friendship, I knew this man was considering his response with some caution, uncertain as to my motives.

"Maybe I'm Kamurro," the man replied, revealing his identity at last. Then he resumed carving a baobab seed pod, a popular pastime among older Aborigines who like to make money from selling their artifacts to tourist shops. Already he had etched in the outlines of a kangaroo hunt across the surface of the nut.

"Is it true that you're a *barnmunji*?" I asked tentatively.

"Who told you about me?" Kamurro's voice was edgy.

"Mr. Rouse. He said you gave him a lot of information about the *rai*."

"That was a long time ago, when things were good 'round here. Now all we do is sit about gettin' drunk."

"But nonetheless the *rai* still exist," I ventured.

"Course they do," Kamurro replied gruffly, rubbing his fingers over the baobab nut.

"And they give you power to see inside a person," I added.

"Mr. Rouse, he tellin' you too much," Kamurro responded cautiously. Yet I could see my interest in the doctrine of the *rai* had aroused him more than he cared to admit.

"Is it also true that you can fly through the air?" I asked.

Kamurro glanced up at me. I was immediately struck by

the change in his manner. The apathy and aggression that had marred his earlier attitude toward me had all but disappeared. Instead a look of grudging complicity had begun to appear on his face.

"I tell you: that missionary fella has been tellin' you too much," he repeated.

Feeling that my presence had been accepted at last, I sat down on the ground opposite Kamurro. Meanwhile the women were watching us from a distance. I could tell they were curious about what was happening because they sent one of their dogs over to investigate. The dog walked up, sniffed my arm, then lay down nearby.

"The women are real busybodies. They want to know what we're talkin' about," Kamurro began with a small smile on his face. "But what they don't know is this dog understands nothin' about the *rai*. The spirits are too clever for 'im.

"Well, we Aboriginal people aren't much without the help of the *rai*," the old man went on. "They're the spirit people who made us. Without them we wouldn't be in this world."

"Not even as a result of a man and woman making love?" I suggested.

"That's white-man talk. Funny business with woman doesn't account for makin' a child. Your people only see things in one way. Always thinkin' 'bout sex," he added. His remark made me recall with some irony Mr. Rouse accusing Aborigines in much the same way.

Kamurro touched his temple and continued:

"The *rai*, they enter a man in his dream because they comin' from the Wandjina. That what important. They hop into a woman's body only after that happens, and make a baby. A man got to see the *rai* in his dream first. Everythin' goes on in our head, not down here." Kamurro patted his thigh to emphasize his point.

I gathered from Kamurro's explanation that in spite of his insistence on the *rai* being spirit entities that wandered about the bush at night, they were also much more. They appeared to be linked to the Wandjina in a spiritual way that could only be invoked in a dream. Physical paternity was so ingrained in my thought, however, that the idea of a person being dreamed into existence confounded me. Yet Kamurro was insistent that the "funny business" between man and woman was incidental to conception. A person was first conceived by the spirit of the *rai* before undergoing a period of physical growth in a woman's womb.

"If the *rai* are responsible for giving everyone life and making people who they are," I replied, "why is it that there are only very few *barnmunji* like yourself around?"

"Not everyone has the right to become a doctor-man. The *rai*, they give us special powers. These powers don't belong to everyone. The *rai* see you as being important. That's why they make me *barnmunji* and not some other fella," Kamurro explained.

"How do the *rai* enter you, and make you a *barnmunji*?"

"Only when the *gedji* crystals are placed inside you. Them spirit stones belongin' to the *rai*."

"Quartz crystals, you mean?"

"*Gedji*, they come from the *rai*," Kamurro insisted. "They don't come from the ground. To become a *barnmunji* you must have your insides taken out your body and replaced with *gedji*. Then the spirit of the *rai* goin' inside you. Once they're in your body you have power, what we call *kurunba*. You become a doctor-man, an expert. The *rai* make it possible for you to see all things. When you go out hunting, you can see through the bushes and know if a kangaroo is there. You can fly, too, that's right! Doctor-men can fly like birds. They can travel under the ground, too, like a lizard. Below the earth he rumbles along just like a *goanna*."

"How can you actually fly?" I asked, finding this revelation a little hard to accept.

"That's a secret," Kamurro replied, not wishing to reveal too much to me. "But I tell you, the *rai*, they teach us, all we know. We can find out what's wrong with a fella when he's feeling sick, too. We look into his body and see the disease shinin' like a light. The healthy parts don't shine like the sick parts. Then we know what's wrong with a fella. The *rai*, they show us how to look inside his body. So for the *rai* to teach us how to fly isn't such a big thing."

"Are you ever called upon to cure people much these days?"

Kamurro glanced down at his baobab nut, as if embarrassed by my question.

"My people don't trust us doctor-men anymore," he said. "They go to white-men doctors in town and get pills. They like to sit in hospital beds and have nurses running around lookin' after them. My people like to have a white fella listen to their insides with something on his ears. A stethoscope, you blokes call it. They don't believe my inner eye can see what's wrong like they did in the old days. Much better than them white doctor-men with their shiny metal ears, anyway."

"Yet in spite of this your people still believe in the *rai*. Even though they go to white doctors, they haven't forgotten the old ways completely," I countered.

"They know they only born because of the *rai*, what's why. We teach them this when they're children. But that doesn't mean they want to listen to what I've got to say anymore."

Kamurro's dilemma was obvious. Not only did he find

himself living on the fringe of white settlement, but it appeared that his skills as a *barnmunji* had been undermined by modern medical practice as a result. Sorcery and magic were no longer acceptable among his people now that they had become mendicants of the state. The old ways were considered to be inferior, little more that the remnants of their wild bush life, which for many Aborigines had become only a memory. To many of them, particularly the younger ones, Kamurro was an argumentative old man, out of touch with modern life.

"My people don't want to believe in my doctor ways because that would mean helpin' themselves. White medicine takes this away from us. It takes away our power," Kamurro added.

"You mean, white medicine and pension checks have stopped your people believing in the old ways," I said.

Kamurro barely nodded.

"*Rai*, they don't like people who don't believe in them. When they die, our people die," he added, a hint of bewilderment in his voice. It was clear that what might happen to his people once they ceased to believe in their culture had only just begun to dawn on him.

I was deeply touched by Kamurro's explanation of his people's logic that transcended any arguments that I might wish to put forth in reply. Here was a man who had seen his culture all but decimated by European settlement in the past 100 years. The power to see with X-ray eyes, to fly through the air like a bird, or walk underground like a lizard—these things were in danger of disappearing from the world forever. I had the impression that Kamurro felt that his culture and beliefs had been irretrievably damaged by the aggressive and often thoughtless ways of white men. Furthermore, the old men like himself were powerless to do anything about it.

"You be careful," he said to me as I climbed onto my bicycle.

"What of?" I asked.

"The *rai*, they got to like you first. Otherwise you be in trouble. They can trip you up pretty quick."

"Thanks for the advice, Kamurro. I'll keep my eyes open," I called as I rode away from the old Aboriginal sorcerer.

Kamurro, meanwhile, picked up his baobab pod and began carving again as if nothing had happened. Clearly the hunting scene he was carving on its surface reminded him of a time when men really did move about with the aid of spirits.

James G. Cowan is an author and poet who has spent much of his life exploring the world of traditional peoples such as the Berbers of Morocco, the Tuareg of the Central Sahara, and the Australian Aborigines. He spent a decade living and traveling in Europe and North America, and then returned to Australia, where he embarked on a series of books and explored the agricultural peoples of early Australia. This story was excerpted from his book, Messengers of the Gods: Tribal Elders Reveal the Ancient Wisdom of the Earth.

PART FOUR

CONSCIOUSNESS

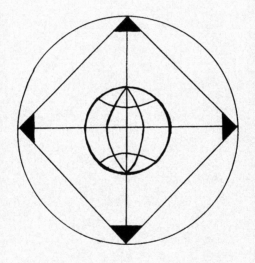

W. PAUL JONES

Trinitarian Thoughts

Everything is connected. Take a look.

HIKING FROM THE SOUTH RIM OF THE GRAND CANYON TO the Colorado River floor is, physically, no major challenge. The most dangerous part is not slipping after an incontinent mule team passes. Many hike it, although those who do the fourteen-mile-round-trip Kaibab Trail in one day may be a more select group. And among these, fewer still attempt the marathon as a spiritual pilgrimage.

My longing to do so began several years earlier when, in a Navajo healing ceremony, I encountered the *"Sipapu."* This small hole in the hogan's floor is a ceremonial focus for the power of the mysterious womb hole from which all spirits are birthed. The real "divine center" is known only to the gods, but many believe it to be the Grand Canyon. Into that huge hole I hiked, the one from which all of us may have come—dust to dust, life to life—on a pilgrimage from sunrise to sunset.

The first half mile was a welcomed contrast to the resort-like atmosphere of the rim. My eyes, at first, were those of the

137

artist. My imagination fashioned a necklace from the maze of switchbacks, stringing together the mellow colors of carefree buttes and pinnacles and palisades. In time, I became more contemplative, emptied of thought, merging and floating with the birds, now at eye level. Other persons must have been so affected, for the map identified a point immediately in front as Buddha Peak, the one to the right as Vishnu Temple. Some time after the third hour, the pilgrimage became decidedly physical and, simultaneously, more spiritual. Thirst was my first clue that I did not belong here. Toads, lizards, a coiled rattlesnake—they all seemed at home—even a vulture overhead, circling with growing interest my slowing steps. A sign put the matter graphically: "Danger! Those without a gallon of water each, turn back now!" Life was as thin as a canteen strap.

With heavy panting, I seemed to be entering the electronic museum display on the rim. It had a beeper that went off every second for three minutes. The total beeps marked the advent of the Canyon within the whole span of time. As I hiked, one fact became increasingly heavy: only with the last beep did the human species appear. In fact, human history is so minuscule that this last beep included not only "us" but all the extinct mammoth animals of prehistory.

To understand what was happening to me, one must understand that I am a theologian, philosophical by training, biblical by choice. History has long been my foundation for theological exploration. But with human figures still visible on the rim, I had quickly walked far beyond the symbolic equivalent of recorded history. And yet, stretching far below me, winding for miles down into the Canyon, strata after strata, stretched endless symbolic layers of a nonhuman time. Billions of years without us. Each of my downward steps was like going back in time a hundred years, as each mile-sign translated beeps into alienation.

It was close to 10 A.M. when I was swept by a childlike thought: *Where was God all this time?* Intellectually, this was no new question. But the artistic eye with which I began, displaced by eyes more contemplative, were now very physical eyes, cutting straight through the romanticism of my theological metaphors. I had to get down and back out by sunset. With night temperatures well below freezing, and my water half gone, conclusions were simple. Lost in this symbolic immensity of time, I as a conscious being was a freak. We simply do not belong.

I picked up a pebble at my feet. The time it reflected, compared with the time in which self-conscious life has been on earth, staggers the mind. In a universe 20 billion years old, the first dated year in history is 4241 B.C. How utterly insignificant to this bleak wholeness is the fact of self-conscious mind. Standing deep within the Canyon, feeling like a humorless afterthought of a mindless whole, my operating assumption as a theologian became a strange non sequitur. How can one any longer take this recent phenomenon of self-consciousness as the image for understanding the meaning of whole? From that point on the trail, I knew myself to be a misfit, for I alone was self-conscious. Impossible to shake was a portrait of the newest kid on the cosmic block, arrogantly insisting that behind everything was one of his kind.

Violating all techniques of suspenseful storytelling, let me just say straight out that I made it down and back in one day. But the price was costly. Merton claimed that in the desert the wrestling with God is until one receives a new name. In the Canyon that day, I knew that my wrestling would be until God, too, was renamed. The irreversibility of this awareness became clear the next day. I drove to Mount Palomar. The conclusion became indelible. Whether I looked into the earth or away from it, the effect was the same. Through that telescope one can see a billion light years away, which is staggering when one remembers that a light year itself is 6 trillion miles. And while our solar system is 7 billion miles in diameter, from outer space it is simply one star in a gigantic galaxy—which itself appears as only a minor smudge with at least 100 million observable galaxies much like our own.

What the Grand Canyon does for time, Palomar does for space. With the arrival of consciousness late on a freaklike speck in an inconceivable vastness, how can one any longer propose self-consciousness as the defining analogy for comprehending the totality? As Freud observed, "I personally have a vast respect for mind, but has nature? Mind is only a little bit of nature, the rest of which seems to be able to get along very well without it."

Existence is the search for the analogy by which to be ordered. A generation ago, Dorothy Emmet concluded that the future of metaphysics (and thus theology) depended upon the emergence of a new analogy capable of igniting the imagination. She recognized, apparently, what is becoming clearer now, that we have crossed a threshold in which deity as self-conscious being can no longer be entertained as anteceding the cosmos. Whatever validity Christianity may claim, it must be in the full face of our cosmic loneliness and the absurd abyss of prior aloneness for any professed deity.

The Canyon, however, focused a second childlike question. If we persist in projecting a self-conscious God as creator-designer of the whole, the question of God's doing becomes even more devastating than God's absence. It was noon when I reached the bottom. Beside the surging Colorado River, I ate a sandwich, watching the pink and orange swirl of clouds stir the Canyon into a cauldron of peach froth, when a motion far closer refocused my eyes. I had been watching the sky through a spider web and in the center was a healthy-sized spider, riding the breeze patiently, oblivious to the peach display. A fly struck the web. With three venomous assaults on the terrorized insect, the spider began sucking it apart, savoring lunch with contentment. How can I stomach a God who designed such an arrangement, especially when, sooner or later, each of us will experience the whole from the vantage point of the fly? The spider may think such an arrangement to be fine, but only until a bird sees its lunch being a spider in the middle of that web. In collecting firewood the previous day, I saw, under a log, what as a child we called "roly-polies." I wondered if they hurt anything. At the Canyon bottom, I knew the absurdity of such a question. There is nothing alive that is not bad news for something. The only image of God that could any longer be viable would be one that permitted me to stare bald-faced at both fly and spider.

Ernest Becker's Pulitzer Prize–winning book, *The Denial of Death*, is deadly to any God who would dare peer out from behind the death and decay woven irradicably into the fabric of "creation." Staring unblinkingly into the repulsive extravagance in time and blood that has brought evolution to where we are, Becker asks, "What are we to make of a creation in which the routine activity is for organisms to be tearing others apart...everyone reaching out to incorporate others who are edible to him?" God cannot be guiltless, whether as the informing "wisdom" of nature's bloody plan or, conceived more distantly, as the force functioning intrusively as "acts of God," specializing in earthquakes and plagues, either willed or permitted. Every attempt at theodicy founders, for any self-conscious deity must be brought to confession by the portrait of a "nightmare spectacular taking place on a planet soaked for hundreds of millions of years in the blood of all its creatures," turning the planet "into a vast pit of fertilizer." A fully conscious creator forces the enigma that confounds every theodicy: the inconceivability of affirming a loving will as having designed a creation in which it is the routine activity of every organism to devour something else for its livelihood. Either we have for this "terror of creation" a Sadomasochistic Designer or an Impotent Watcher or else we must forfeit primal self-consciousness as our informing image. Teresa of Avila was enough of a mystic to put it charitably, "I do not wonder, God, that you have so few friends from the way you treat them."

The Grand Canyon is indeed a cauldron of death, symbol of creation's bloody chalice. Its restless sides teem with life, propelled by an insatiable drive to endure, indeed, to prevail. Wind, river, clutching root-fingers of trees, lean varmints in crouched determination—all are sisters-brothers in the surging restlessness. We can feel this straining deeply within ourselves. Life is thrashing about, expanding, reaching out, in uncertain directions for seemingly unknown reasons. But here one can sense strangely that consciousness is not alien, but a breakthrough—within and for the whole. Ironically, while such emergence brings the alienating burden of knowing what nothing else in creation seems yet to know, it opens the religious threshold: greeting self-consciousness as the emergence of the whole.

W. Paul Jones has taught at Yale, Princeton, and St. Paul School of Theology, and has published widely both in journals and books. He alternates life in the inner city with being a Trappist monk. He has five daughters, which is quite interesting for a Roman Catholic priest. The last mountain he and his daughters climbed was Chair Mountain near Marble, Colorado.

JAMES D. HOUSTON

* * *

Sandbath Resurrection

*Two dislocated souls search for home and find it
in the black sands of Kyushu.*

KAGOSHIMA IS THE SOUTHERNMOST CITY IN JAPAN, AND WE
had not planned to go beyond it. But somewhere in our travels another American had told us we should look at Ibusuki,
down at the lower end of the last peninsula on the island of
Kyushu. The town was small, this woman said, and cheap, and
close to the water, and warm most of the year, which is something to think about as fall turns to winter. It was the kind of
thing that happens when you are on your way from Point A
to Point B and you meet someone on a subway platform who
has just come back from Point X, a place you've never heard
of or thought of visiting, but a few days later there you are,
wandering into an unknown town for reasons that are still not
entirely clear.

House hunting, we told ourselves, as we walked out of
the depot, hailed a cab, and taxied over to a low-budget inn
we'd found in the pamphlet that comes with the Rail Pass.
House hunting, we said again the next morning—though
each day now it was harder to fight down the growing sense

of dislocation. By that time we had moved in and out of too many inns and hotels and cabs and train stations. The bags were getting heavier, and after two weeks on this gypsy path, the quest, the adventure, the challenge of Japan was wearing thin. This country was too strange, and perhaps more trouble than it was worth.

As I woke the next morning I was having the second thoughts, or third thoughts, that can grip you in the early days of a long trip, when you begin to fear the whole expedition may be a terrible mistake. Remembering all the loose ends and unfinished business I'd left behind, I woke in the predawn of Ibusuki thinking, "What's going on? A week ago we had never heard of this place. And what am I really doing over here seven time zones away from my phone and my desk and my work and my stuff, all my carefully assembled time and stuff?"

Well, as they often say, when you are ready for the answer, the question will appear. And the answer was about to present itself, there in the strangest of all the strange places we had seen.

In this land of the unexpected, Ibusuki is the farthest from what we had expected to find. It does not resemble any of the Japans you see promoted or publicized. There are no world-class shrines or gardens. You don't find Kabuki there or sumo wrestling or cherry trees in bloom. There is no fast-track urban life, no sidewalk multitude streaming toward the underground trains. It was October. The streets were almost empty—a few honeymooning couples, a few elderly retirees, a few off-season sightseers from China and Korea. In the yards around the houses we saw a lot of cactus, and bushes of red hibiscus. Palm trees lined the boulevards, royal palms, date palms, palms with the spiky leaves Hawaiians use to make *lauhala* matting. The latitude is more southerly than San

Diego, in line with northern Baja. Later a fellow from Tokyo who has been to the U.S. would tell us, with a condescending city smile, "That part of Kyushu is what you might call the Alabama of Japan."

At the southern end of the island, two long peninsulas, like two facing crab claws, form Kagoshima Bay. Ibusuki lies inside this bay, on the protected inner edge of the peninsula called Satsuma, with a view across still waters toward the worn-down cliffs of former craters, now green and razor edged, much like the cliffs that line the north shore of the Hawaiian island of Kaua'i. Maybe this in itself has prepared me to surrender, something about the Polynesian look of the volcanic land-scape that shaped the glassy bay, the steeply eroded peaks, the palms, the blue water lapping porous lava rocks.

After a morning of halfhearted apartment pricing, we do what Japanese heat seekers travel hundreds of miles to do and stroll over to the bath house, where steam from subterranean springs comes percolating right up through the sand. For 300 yen you get a locker and a clean *yukata*, a long robe, blue on white. You can't wear anything underneath, says the woman who takes the money. "All off. No underpants. Nothing."

Inside the locker room you strip and don the robe and feel the crisp, freshly ironed cotton on your skin. (Half an hour later it will be dark with sweat and with the fine black sand you carry back to the bath house where you'll drop it in a soggy heap with all the other spent *yukata*, then shower off the sand and soap down and shower again and slide into *furo*—the tile-lined tub filled with mineral water piped from the springs—for the finishing work, the final polish.)

Outside the bath house door rubber thongs, *zori*, are piled in a heap, several dozen, of varying sizes. We each grab a cou-ple of these and clop along the concrete walkway, looking out across the dark sand turned black by wetness. Steam curls from the low-tide flats, much as it rises from the vents and fissures in the floor of Kilauea Caldera on the Big Island of Hawai'i. An important difference is that here the bonneted women await you, shovels in hand, standing by their rows of shallow graves.

We stretch out in the sand, attended by these shovel-bearing women, and one leans in so close to me, her eyes gazing into mine with an intimacy so tender, so disarming, I have to relax. I have to surrender. She wraps the white towel around my head and gently pulls it snug beneath my chin. She does not speak. She steps back and throws the first shovelful across my shoulder, black and hot and wet enough that it does not spread. Each grain seems to lie where it lands, making weight against the skin. The next shovelful lands on my belly, the next on my hips. Soon she has me buried to my neck, the dark sand pressing along my body, and steam rising through the sand beneath me, from the hot springs. Only my head shows, one head in a row of towel-wrapped heads lined along the black sand beach.

She looks to be about sixty. She wears the clothes of a country woman dressed for field work, baggy blue trousers, white apron, blue bonnet. She laughed when she saw me coming, laughed at my height. She spoke to the other women, all dressed alike, all carrying long-handled shovels, and they all laughed as she trenched an extra foot of sand so I could stretch at full length and join the others staring at the sky.

Now she leans on her shovel, and I am breathing slowly under the weight of all the sand, while the heat cooks my neck, my legs, my back. The women move away to meet some new arrivals who have walked down from the bath house. I close my eyes. For the first time in two weeks I feel at ease, at rest. Why? Is it just the sand and the beach air and the heat of this outdoor Asian sauna? Something I'd been barely aware of is being steamed away, some deep anxiety is dissolving, floating upward with the whispers of the moisture and the heat. For the first time since we landed in Japan, I feel connected. But how? And why here?

I doze.

The lap-lap of tiny waves revives me. My nose revives me. Both together. Splashing surf and itching nose. I cannot scratch. My arms and hands are buried. My eyes begin to itch. My chin. My neck. Suddenly each second is a little test of the will. I can force my arms upward through the sand to scratch away at my face and eyes, but that would break the crust, break open the cocoon of heat, break the spell.

I concentrate on voices. Whose are they? From Jeanne, from other towel-surrounded heads along the beach I hear nothing but the occasional intake—Ssssssss—a stoic hissing through the teeth, a long exhale. The voices come from the women with the shovels. Softly they chatter, in words I can't comprehend, as they move the sand around, smoothing, preparing it. I listen while the minutes pass. I can't say how many minutes. Two. Or ten. I listen until my itching subsides, and the nearby scratch of a shovel digging—chk...chk... chk—is a gentle drumbeat calling me back to life.

It is the same woman, in her blue cotton trousers, white apron to her knees. She is working right next to me, clearing another space. She glances my way. Again our eyes meet, just a glimpse, an instant, and here at last I find the touchpoint—after two weeks of dislocated gypsy roaming—a first point of entry into this unknown and foreign land.

It is not the town of Ibusuki that touches me. We'll be out of here and on our way tomorrow afternoon. The touchpoint is located somewhere else. It is in the dark sand. It is inside the earth and the steam. It is in the eyes of this unnamed woman gazing out from under the brim of her white, farm-country bonnet. Sweat is pouring off my face, into the towel. I am cooking in my sweat, inside the wet cotton skin of my *yukata*. My back is stinging with the slow burn of steady heat you know is going to be good for you. And what comes rising through me, along with the heat, is a liberating form of knowledge, or perhaps memory—that the land is not foreign. It is familiar. This is the sand and the steam and the subsoil and the hot spring and the mountain peninsula of the globe we all inhabit. And the look in the eyes of this woman is familiar too. You would recognize it anywhere. She is the tender-eyed lover, and the mother tucking you in at night, and the one who has come to bury you so that you can be born again.

James D. Houston is the author of seven novels, including Snow Mountain Passage, Continental Drift, *and* The Last Paradise, *which received a 1999 American Book Award. Among his several nonfiction works is* In The Ring of Fire: A Pacific Basin Journey, *from which this story was excerpted. He and his wife, Jeanne Wakatsuki Houston, live in Santa Cruz, California.*

SEAN O'REILLY

✶ ✶ ✶

St. Peter's Black Box

An apostate is humbled.

THE PLAZA IN FRONT OF ST. PETER'S BASILICA IN ROME imposes itself on the imagination. It is humbling to stand at the religious center of 2,000 years of creative and passionate spiritual endeavor. Here in the presence of the unthinkable successor to the mighty Roman Empire, the mind tends to implode, to shift into reverie and things besides mere thoughts enter the heart. So much history in one place creates a kind of soul warp where the collective consciousness of untold generations creates images in the mind and leaves the vision slightly blurred to accommodate the intrusion. One staggers through this psychic doorway to discover that nothing is as it seems.

I was a second year student in the University of Dallas Rome program. We were to spend three days a week in class and the rest of the time roaming Europe. We went just about everywhere—Paris, the coast of Spain, Germany, Austria, Switzerland, and even North Africa but it was in Rome that I experienced the unusual.

The first thing that I noticed after entering the Basilica of St. Peter's and gaping about were the confessional lights bright against dark wood, then the signs in many languages above the confessional boxes. They seemed forbidding and ritual-encrusted, archaic technology left over from a vanished yet still vital world. I was reminded of an old science fiction definition of a "black box": a mechanism of unknown workings which produces mysterious results.

Confessions were being heard in Spanish, English, Chinese, Malay, Polish, Czech, Russian, and God knows how many other tongues. I thought to myself, "How convenient, anyone could go." Immediately, I mentally countered with the thought that it would be convenient for those who wanted to go—myself of course not being included. I could not tear myself away, however, and for some reason I kept looking at the lights. I then forcibly walked the other way, thinking that there would be many other interesting things to look at. I wandered over to the Pieta and marveled at the flow of the marble. (Only the real masters can make marble look like human flesh close up. The work of Praxiteles comes to mind and the stunning statue of Antinous at Delphi—small wonder that Hadrian had been so captivated by him.)

After a few minutes with Michelangelo, I found myself back in the same place. I started to become annoyed. What bullshit! Who could need confession? I was surprised that this was even an issue for me, as I had left the Catholic Church at fourteen and at twenty-one had no intention of returning. I was suddenly caught in the gravitation of the struggle that was going on and recognized that I was in fact having an argument with myself. It was one of those rare moments when you catch yourself looking at yourself and wondering what the problem is.

From this illumined perspective, desires—whether for good

or ill—are transparently clear. You either want something or you do not. I experienced what in retrospect might be called a paradigm shift. I caught myself denying what appeared to be a bizarre desire (from my perspective at the time) and simultaneously realized from an entirely different and larger perspective that what I wanted was tantalizing and possibly beneficial in a way I could not understand.

I knew at that point that I had to go into the confessional—there was no honest way out. I simply wanted to go and there was no denying it. I felt a subtle shuddering as if I was standing at the edge of a cliff and there was no turning back. At the same time there was an immense clarity to what I was about to do. The fulfillment of my own history, a venture into the unknown, a vast quantum leap into the future seemed to be at hand. I hesitated; what sins would I confess? The answer bore down on me with awful certainty. "Confess all of them." I realized that if I was going to do this, there was no point in doing it halfway.

So I went in and confessed all my misdeeds from age fourteen to twenty-one—a seven-year accumulation of sexual misconduct and a host of other failings. I do not remember all that I confessed or even what the priest was like but I do remember stumbling out of the confessional like a person facing a new dawn after a reprieve from some long incarceration. I felt lighter and also re-oriented—as if something had been out of focus and was now suddenly much clearer. I immediately wrote it off to psychological relief but could not quite escape the sense that something extraordinary had happened.

My life was never the same after that. I had many moral lapses from that day on but always went back to confession, and astoundingly, the relief from spiritual oppression and darkness always seemed to occur. If I had to describe it another way, I would say that before I go to confession, I feel fragmented, vaguely depressed, somewhat inverted and upon receiving the forgiveness of Christ, set aright or made joyfully whole in a mysterious manner. What is certain is that in Rome, St. Peter's black box opened a window onto a different reality for me.

Sean O'Reilly is editor-at-large for Travelers' Tales and has co-edited such books as The Road Within, Pilgrimage, The Ultimate Journey, *and* Testosterone Planet. *He is also the author of* How to Manage Your DICK: Redirect Sexual Energy and Discover Your More Spiritually Enlightened, Evolved Self.

CHARLES NICHOLL

✦ ✦ ✦

Moonsong and Martin Luther

In northern Thailand, a former tuk-tuk
*driver tells the story of Buddha and Mara
to the author and his Thai friend.*

KATAI AND I MET THE OLD MONK, IN THE BIG OPEN-SIDED
sala of Wat Pa Sak. We sat beneath a large gilded Buddha in
the sleek etiolated, Burmese-influenced style of Lan Na. His
name was Moonsong. He was a thin, knotty, myopic man. He
said he was seventy but he looked younger. He was unshaven,
his orange robe creased and tattered, his heavy spectacles cel-
lotaped at the hinges. He had once been a *tuk-tuk* driver in
Bangkok. He showed us an old photo: a tough bare-chested
man leaning against the door of a repair shop. It's odd how
the monk's robe seems to partition the wearer off from "normal" life, so one is surprised at this secular past. He had gone
into the monkhood twelve years ago, seven of those spent as
a novice.

Did he prefer being a monk?

"Of course." Then, with a little laugh, "Most of the time."

He was keen to practice his English. He taught English to
the temple boys of the locality. There were certain rather
specialist points he wanted me to explain to him. On the

blackboard in the *sala* I defined as best I could the distinction between angels and fairies. I corrected his impression that Martin Luther was a "famous English monk," and that Henry VIII had murdered him. I said he was thinking of Thomas à Becket and Henry II. Luther is a well-known figure in Thai religious circles, because he opposed a corrupt and mercenary clergy, and because, as Moonsong now put it, "he taught that God was inside us, not"—he gestured to the raftered roof of the *sala*—"up there. So it is with Buddhism. It is just following the good inside you, and putting aside"—an effortful pushing-away gesture—"the bad."

I said, "It is difficult to put aside the bad."

"Of course," he said quickly, a touch of irritation in the reedy voice. "Of course. The spirit of Mara is always ready to make trouble. But look." He gestured up at the bronzed Buddha above us. "You see our Buddha here. He is seated on Mara. Mara is all that you wish for, all you desire. The Buddha has risen above this, and now he may sit in meditation on top of Mara."

Mara was in the form of a serpent coiled up like a cushion beneath Buddha. I remembered Katai talking of the *naga* performing this office for the Buddha, and asked if they were the same.

"Mara is much greater," said Moonsong. "The evils of water brought by the *naga* are perhaps a part of Mara's work, but the *naga* brings the good things of water too. No, Mara is *phanyaa mahn*, the Prince of Demons. If you do not know it, I will tell you the story of Buddha and Mara."

We settled at his feet, which were dusty and crooked.

"When our Buddha attained to truth beneath the bodhi tree, Mara gathered an army of demons to bring fear to him. Mara rode at the head of the army on his war elephant, Giri Mekhala. But the goddess of the earth, who we call Nang

Thoranee, saw that the Buddha was about to be engulfed by demons. She squeezed all the waters from her hair and sent down a flood to drown the demons.

"So next, Mara sent a plague of rats to devour the holy scriptures. The Buddha created at that moment the first cat in the world. She is called Phaka Waum. She chased away the rats, and preserved the truth of the Buddha's teaching, and to this day we consider it a great wrong to kill a cat.

"Now Mara hurled his most terrible weapon, a great thunderbolt, but the Buddha caught it in his hand, and there and then he turned it into a garland of flowers, like the *puang malai* you see hanging on his neck now.

"Last, Mara sent his three daughters to tempt the Buddha. His three daughters are Aradi, discontent; Tanha, desire; and Raka, love. Well, this was the hardest fight for Buddha, because now he was fighting the dangers inside himself. But the Buddha resisted their charms, and so today we say: the power of dharma—the truth of the Buddha—can save us from all the dangers inside us and around us.

"So, yes, of course it is difficult to put aside the spirit of Mara. We must learn to turn our desires into beautiful flowers. We must learn to place ourselves above Mara, like the Buddha does. Not only so that we can be above Mara, but so that we can see the dangers. They are outside us: desires and discontents. They are no longer part of us."

"They are part of life."

"Yes, in one sense. But we Buddhists say, rather they are part of death. They are part of the world that dies. Mara is a principle of death. That is why he is not the same as *naga*. The *naga* is dangerous, but he is a principle of life. In the Festival of Lights in Thailand, the Loi Kratong, it is said that it was a king of the *naga*, Phra Upagota, who finally helped to capture and conquer Mara. This was in the time of King

Asoka, who brought the Theravada teachings of Buddhism into Thailand."

"But aren't desire and discontent a principle of life too?" I persisted.

His lined face looked down at me, a little rabbit-toothed pout. He said cryptically, "After noon a monk may not eat, but he may take water any time."

"I don't understand."

"Food is what you want, water is what you need."

He went still for a moment, eyes focused on something beyond us, mouth still showing two yellow teeth. I started to say something, but Katai laid a hand on my arm, and put a finger to her lips.

I heard the leisurely rattle of a dried-up teak leaf tumbling from the tall canopy. The temple was called Wat Pa Sak because 200 teak trees had gone into making its enclosure.

After a bit he looked at me and smiled. "Your Luther says: *Pecca fortiter, sed fortius fide.* Sin strongly, but believe more strongly. I think that is a good beginning for us all."

He climbed wearily to his feet, and began to rummage in a wooden chest near by. He brought out a little medallion: a tiny tin Buddha inside a triangular blob of perspex. Katai said, "It is a *phra kliang* to hang around your neck."

I made a *wai* and took it from him. Katai too made a *wai*, and I got the feeling she was thanking him for what he had done to "enlighten" me, a poor *farang* who knew nothing. Phra Moonsong received our thanks with a slight bow, but no *wai*.

Katai said quietly, "He would like you to give money for the temple." I handed some notes to him. She too gave him money, but she placed the notes on top of the wooden chest. A monk may not take anything directly from a woman's hand.

"Thank you," Moonsong said, "for teaching me about Martin Luther, and about Thomas the Becket. I shall tell my pupils." He thought for a moment. "So. Is it right: 'Who will rid me of this turbulent priest'?"

"Perfect," I said.

He grinned, impish, pedantic. "Never perfect," he said. He ambled off. At the edge of the *sala*, where its shade met the shimmer of the midday light, he met another monk. They conversed for a moment, a faint breeze catching their robes, a few more teak leaves slowly falling, and then they went their separate ways.

Charles Nicholl is the author of The Reckoning, The Fruit Palace, *and* Borderlines: A Journey in Thailand and Burma, *from which this story was excerpted. He lives with his wife and four children in Hereford, England.*

JAN MORRIS

Chaurikharka

*A weary traveler is nurtured
in a simple mountain home.*

ALL OF US KNOW PLACES—ASPECTS OF PLACES EVEN—WHOSE
memory can trigger in us haunting sensations of happiness,
sadness, or plain nostalgia. For me their epitome is
Chaurikharka, which is a speckle of small huts, encouched in
gardens and potato fields, somewhere in the Himalayan
foothills of east Nepal. I can find it on no map, and it appears
in none of the travelers' tales because it is not on the way to
anywhere in particular, contains nothing very startling, and is
inhabited only by quiet Sherpa people. Yet the very name of
the place, so exotic, so mellifluous on the tongue and so dev-
ilishly hard to spell, summoned up in me a mood of lyrical and
slightly mystical serenity.

I was ill when I went there. Trekking down from Namche
Bazaar in the company of a Sherpa named Sonam, I was
suddenly felled by a combination, I suppose, of fatigue, excitement, altitude sickness, and a somewhat cavalier attitude of
hygiene. Sonam immediately invited me to spend a few days
in his own home. It was only a few miles off the way, he said,
and he and his family would see me through my fever.

Sonam's house in my recollection was darker, smokier, and more mysterious than other homes. This is perhaps because he rolled out my sleeping bag for me in the room that was also the family temple, with a dozen small images of the Buddha, attended by butter candles, gleaming at the other end. The room was warm, woody, creaky, smoke blackened, and through its shadows I could always see those gently smiling images, flickered by their candlelight.

Outside the house everything steamed. The monsoon was upon us. The rains fell heavily for several hours each day, and the gardens that surrounded Chaurikharka's houses were all lush and vaporous. My room had no window, but the open door looked out upon the Sonam family plot, and from it there came a fragrance so profoundly blended of the fertile and the rotten, the sweet and the bitter, the emanations of riotous growth and the intimations of inevitable decay, that still, if ever my mind wanders to more sententious subjects, I tend to smell the vegetable gardens of Chaurikharka.

The taste of the potatoes, too, roasted at the family hearth, seemed to me almost philosophically nourishing, while the comfort of the powerful white liquor, *rakshi*, with which the Sonams now and then dosed me, and the merry voices of the children, frequently hushed lest they disturb my convalescence, and the kind, wondering faces of the neighbors who occasionally looked through the open door, and the clatter of the rain on the roof and the hiss of it in the leaves outside, and the enigmatic smiles of those small golden figures in their half light at the end of the room—all built up in my mind an impression not just of peace and piquancy, but of holiness.

Mind you, it is all a blur to me. During all my time in Sonam's house I was in a baffled state of mind. This is partly because I was sick, but partly because I did not know then, as I do not know now, precisely where Chaurikharka was. It seemed in my fancy to be somewhere altogether alone in that wide and marvelous wilderness. One of the great Himalayan peaks rose to the north of us, white as Heaven itself, but I never knew which. A little river rushed through the gully below the house, rocky and slate gray, but I have no idea what its name was, or where it was going. When we left to resume our march to Kathmandu, Sonam took me, still in a kind of daze, back to the wide trail which led from the Sherpa country to the central valley of Kathmandu, but whether we had been to east or west of it, north or south, I was never entirely sure. Chaurikharka might have been an invented place, dreamed up by kindly necromancers to restore me.

Was it? Have I invented it myself? Not, I promise you, in the fact. Chaurikharka exists all right, somewhere out there, and I really did go there with Sonam. Every place, like every experience, is both active and passive. It gives to you, and you also give to it, so that its meaning is specific to you alone. Others might have found in Chaurikharka stimulants, depressants perhaps, of altogether different kinds; it is out of my particular sensibility that my own image of it comes—my need to match its fulfillment, my distress to fit its solace, my sickness to find its cure in that quiet darkened room. So it is that I carry my Chaurikharka wherever I go, frequently sensing the hot steamy damp of its fields as I lean from my window at home, and remembering the silent Buddhas among their candles, when the softer rain of Gwynedd spatters my roof.

Jan Morris is the author of more than forty books, and her essays on travel are classics of the genre. What she has called her final book, Trieste and the Meaning of Nowhere, *was published in 2001. Her first book,* Coast to Coast *(written in 1955), has just been rereleased as a Travelers' Tales Classic. This story was excepted from* Pleasures of a Tangled Life. *She lives in Wales.*

PART FIVE

ENCOUNTER

BRETT HARRIS

_⋆ [⋆] _⋆

Restless Ghost

Who you gonna call?

THE WITCH DOCTOR PLACED HIS HAND ON MY TREMBLING shoulder and assured me I would be safe. "Mister, don't be scared. Fatima only attacks women. She's not interested in you." Meanwhile, my adopted sister was semiconscious on the living room couch, sweating profusely and speaking in tongues.

"Besides," he continued, "this sort of thing is common. It's nothing to get excited about."

Is it common for a woman to be possessed by a vindictive ghost? Well, that depends on where you are. I was in Sulawesi, living with an affluent Indonesian family that consisted of my Ibu (mother), Bapak (father), and two bright and engaging teenage sisters—Sari and Wati. Like most things in Indonesia, my introduction to the spirit world occurred over food.

It was a normal evening. I ate my dinner of *sambal*, rice, and spicy fish, as the rest of the family watched television.

After taking a few bites, though, I suddenly noticed a strange, eerie silence in the house. For the first time since my arrival three months earlier, the entire family was quiet. Titi, the normally chirping pet cockatoo, held his beak shut. The cats were completely still, and my sisters were not engaging in their normal evening-time gossip. Even the volume of the constantly blaring television set seemed subdued.

Then, in the space of about two seconds, something extraordinary happened. The cats screeched at the top of their lungs, Titi began to squawk, and Wati let out a quick, high-pitched, blood-curdling yelp before passing out on the couch.

I was stunned, but the rest of the family didn't even seem surprised. Bapak gently laid Wati down and put her head on a pillow while Ibu took out prayer beads and chanted some mysterious Arabic incantations, continuously stroking Wati's hair. Sari got some rubbing lotion. All of them appeared concerned, but not overly so. Rather than a pressing emergency, I felt they were going through a normal, though troubling, routine.

Suddenly, Wati opened her eyes. Except, she wasn't Wati.

Her dilated pupils shone with a harsh glare, and my sister's normally pleasant face had dissolved into a hard mask of stern, unyielding features. She opened her mouth, groaned, and then collapsed again into unconsciousness.

Bewildered, I finally regained my voice. "What's going on?" The family, oblivious to me until now, turned around, startled. Sari spoke first. "Don't worry, Brett. This happens from time to time. It's, it's…" She looked around nervously for help.

My mother laughed reassuringly. "It's a ghost, Brett. But don't be concerned, she only likes women. She won't attack you." Rather than provide the relief that was intended, it heightened my worries. "A ghost? There's a ghost?" I could feel my face turning white.

Wati was lying down peacefully now, and Ibu began to rub

lotion on her temples, chanting prayers under her breath. Bapak picked up the telephone and walked into the kitchen. Sari answered my question.

"About two years ago, Wati went on a trip to Selajar, an island south of here. While she was there, she disrupted this evil spirit's grave. Ever since then, the ghost refuses to leave Wati alone. But don't worry, Brett. It's no big deal. Most people get possessed from time to time." I remembered what I had learned in my orientation training back in the States. It had included such laughably profound gems as "Don't judge your host culture," and "Try to understand things from their point of view." Their point of view? It's normal to be possessed by a ghost? I tried to come up with a different theory. Maybe Wati was having a seizure or heart palpitations. Maybe it was a severe mental illness. She certainly wasn't faking.

All I could stammer was, "Does this happen often?" My father entered the room to hang up the telephone. He exchanged glances with Ibu. They seemed more worried about me being upset than their daughter being unconscious. Bapak turned toward me. "This is the third time for Wati. But don't worry, Brett, I'm sure the ghost will go back to Selajar soon. I just spoke with the *dukun*. He'll help Wati get rid of this intruder." Meanwhile, my sister seemed to be resting comfortably, though her lips moved, shaping words with no sound.

Although I was worried about Wati, I was excited about meeting a witch doctor face-to-face. I hoped to see a real exorcism with holy water, chants, fire, and other eye-popping special effects. I expected an iron-willed old man, his body etched with tattoos and perhaps a bone through his hair, ready to do bloody battle with the spirit world. Instead, about an hour later, a skinny young man wearing an "Alien Nation" t-shirt and Levi's jeans knocked on the front door. With his baby face, he seemed barely out of high school, though I later found out that he was twenty-seven and considered a junior *dukun*. His boss was busy and would come that evening if there were any serious problems. I noticed his motorcycle had a "Nirvana" bumper sticker on its fender and almost asked him if Kurt Cobain was working on anything new. Maybe a duet with Jimi Hendrix? As he walked in, the *dukun* noticed my worried expression, which contrasted so completely with the rest of the family. He tried to reassure me. "Don't worry, mister. Spirits usually stay away from white people." While I was deciding whether to be relieved or insulted, the young *dukun* went up to Wati and began massaging oils into her skin. This semiwakened her and they began to speak softly. She spoke a strange language, full of grunts and hisses, which only the visitor seemed to understand.

"She is speaking Bahasa Ambon, the language of ancient Moluccas," Sari whispered to me.

After a few moments, Wati collapsed again and the *dukun* turned to the family.

"It's Fatima again. She didn't go back to Selajar like I instructed her last time because she is still angry with Wati." He sighed. "This woman has had a very bad life—and a very bad afterlife. When she was a child, the Portuguese captured her at home in the Moluccas. She was transported to Ternate, where she served as a slave for at least fifteen years. Then, without warning, she was put onboard another ship. Perhaps to work somewhere else. She doesn't know." He shrugged. "Fatima's ship was wrecked off the coast of Selajar. Because she had no burial and no one to remember her, this poor woman has been wandering around that island for over four hundred years. I think I can convince Fatima to leave, at least for a while, and then Wati will have to learn some spiritual exercises to strengthen her defenses."

I was spellbound, but my family just nodded like he had diagnosed the flu. "Like I told you last time," the *dukun* continued, "the most important news is that this is not a very dangerous ghost. She's just an ordinary spirit. Though she might be trying to have a little fun, Fatima will not kill Wati. She'll leave as soon as she gets bored.

After giving this reassurance, the *dukun* went back to work on my sister. He carefully positioned sweet-smelling incense and lumps of black dirt in strategic locations around the room. Then he leaned over the couch, rubbed Wati's head, and chanted some Arabic prayers. The entire ceremony was subdued and quiet. Slowly, my sister's eyes opened and she looked hazily out at the rest of us. Ibu went to get her some water while Bapak walked the *dukun* out. As he left, the *dukun* turned to me. "I know white people are usually very scared of ghosts, so maybe I shouldn't tell you this." Curious, I moved in closer.

"I was surprised, since this sort of spirit usually only likes women. However, she was very interested in you. In fact, Fatima asked me about you several times. She said that you remind her of her Portuguese master. As you can imagine, she didn't like you very much." He started his motorcycle and laughed. "I wouldn't worry, though. She probably won't bother you at all."

Probably? For the next few weeks, I slept with the lights on. However, Fatima was never heard from again.

At least, not yet.

Brett Harris is an economist who served a two-year stint with the East-West Center in Honolulu.

ROBERT GOLLING JR.

⋆ ⋆ ⋆

A World Without Latkes

The author finds continuity and history in a simple dish.

ON A FLIGHT TO CHICAGO I SETTLED INTO MY SEAT LOCATED on the left side of the plane, on the aisle. I was looking forward to a good solid block of reading time. A steady stream of people bumped their way down the aisle, finding seats, looking for carry-on luggage space. A lady with a Nordstrom bag smiled at me. "Oh, thank you," the lady said as I stood out of her way. She slipped across my row to the window seat. "So many people have no manners these days, thank you." I helped her bag into the overhead storage.

Plumpish, not fat, she looked to be in her late fifties or early sixties. Her face was round with hints of wrinkles next to her mouth and eyes. She wore an exercise suit that was dark blue with large white stripes on the jacket. The material was of some crinkly, shiny fabric. Beneath the jacket she wore a dark red blouse. A thin gold chain flashed around her neck, diamond studs glittered on her ears. She wore white tennis shoes. Practical traveling wear; the effect was fancy casual.

She settled into her seat and I back into mine. "Good

morning," she said. Trying not to be too friendly and display-
ing my book, "Good morning," I said; but I couldn't help but
smile as I saw her perched next to the window, wiggling to get
comfortable before take off.

"My name is Esther." Her right hand was undeniable as she
grabbed just the fingers of my right hand. "I'm Bob." I got the
feeling that the next four hours were not going to be my own.

"Would you like a Tic Tac?" she offered. As I declined she
began a monologue. She'd been out visiting her daughter in
San Jose, California. "Where do you live Bob?...Campbell? Is
that near by?" She was on her way home now. She'd had to
take a taxi; the daughter and son-in-law were at work; she
didn't mind. "You're going to Chicago on business? Oh, training for your company."

It wasn't a frantic jabber, but a kind of continuous chatter.
Like air is for breathing, for Esther, words were always in her
mouth. "I transfer in Chicago. My home is in Allentown,
Pennsylvania..." She told me about her husband, Jerry. He
owned a small furniture store; he was always working; she
didn't mind.

Being curious and courteous, I had been looking at her
over my left shoulder. "Oh, Esther, I have to turn away. I have
a cramp in my neck." I said. "That's O.K." she said and continued on. She'd left a week's worth of dinners frozen for Jerry.
"He'll eat the meat loaf and the latkes," she said "but he won't
touch the casseroles."

"Latkes?" I asked. I had heard of them, but I wasn't quite
sure what they were. Like one of those words you vaguely
know in context, but when asked to define you are at a loss.
So was I with latkes.

"Latkes?" she looked slightly incredulous and bemused. "A
simple dish, really, made from nothing. A treat. They're a traditional Chanukah dish. Pancakes, that's all they are. Latke

means pancake in Yiddish. They are made with potatoes, onions, salt and pepper, or just about anything else you want to throw in. Fried golden brown, topped with sour cream and applesauce. They're like a dessert. A world without latkes is a world without light." As she spoke a look of great distance and time came over her face.

Even though my neck hurt like hell there was something more I wanted to find out about Esther and latkes. What was that look about? Stretching and rubbing my neck I asked, "So tell me, Esther, about latkes and light."

"Would you like to know?" one eyebrow arched. "Oh, I should be cooking them for you. Some people, they're such purists they won't change a thing. True, there are certain stages…well, if you don't do them right the latkes won't turn out as good; but you can do lots of different things too."

"Start with potatoes. Everybody has potatoes. In the old days that's all you had to eat. My mother, God rest her soul, always insisted, grate the potatoes with the small holes on the grater, and the onions with the large holes. But I've used a food processor and it works just fine. Into a bowl first grate onions then potatoes, then onions, then potatoes, and so on. You do this so the potatoes don't turn brown. A little lemon juice doesn't hurt either. Drain as much water as possible into a bowl. This is key, the less water the better. After a while a sediment will settle into the bottom of the bowl. Pour off the water, and add the sediment back into the potatoes and onions."

Esther was so animated telling me her recipe I could almost see her bustling about in her kitchen. I imagined the phone to her ear. Talking, talking, talking as she grated, poured, and squeezed. Maybe a neighbor sat at the kitchen table drinking tea and kibitzing.

"The traditional way, Mama always insisted, is to add flour or matzoth meal, a couple of slightly beaten eggs, salt and pepper, and that's all. Then you just fry them up quick as that. Aaaahh, but what is life without a little spice. Look around your kitchen. Aunt Birdie used to add bits of mushrooms and a little garlic."

I nodded my head thinking that anything else you could do to potatoes would probably be good on latkes. Nodding my head helped relieve the cramp in my neck.

"Aunt Birdie?" I asked.

"Mama's youngest sister, her name was Bertha. But my sisters and I called her Birdie. She was small and used to eat little amounts, a cracker, a piece of cheese, a slice of apple all throughout the day. She was always eating but she never gained a pound. We were never allowed to call her Birdie. It was our private name for her. Now it doesn't matter."

"No, why not?" I asked.

"They've passed on. My sisters too. They're all gone now," she said.

"I'm sorry." My apology seemed not enough, but it was the best I could do.

"It's O.K.," she said "It was all a long time ago."

We sat quietly for awhile. I had recently lost my mother to cancer. Our respective losses, except for time, seemed the same. "How much flour should I use with how many potatoes and onions?" I asked.

"Portions shmortions, who knows from portions? It's been so long since I looked at a recipe. Use three or four potatoes, one onion, one slightly beaten egg and one half cup flour until mixed up it looks like applesauce, salt and pepper to taste. Then add what ever spice you like. Parsley is good. Garlic, basil, and parmesan gives you a real pesto flavor."

"I like pesto," I said thinking pine nuts would be good in them also. "What about cooking them?"

"To cook them, first heat your pan, then add one-quarter

inch of oil. Use good vegetable oil. This is how latkes are connected to Chanukah. Oil is light."

"Oil?" I asked.

"Yes, Chanukah is the celebration of a great Maccabean victory that rescued Judaism from annihilation. Judah the Maccabee celebrated the victory by lighting the lamps of a great menorah. In those days their lamps were fueled by oil. So heat your oil, medium-high heat, spoon out and flatten a latke, a few minutes on each side, until golden brown. That's all it takes."

She continued telling about this person or that relative that had used zucchini, sweet potatoes, or dill with cucumber/yogurt sauce. As she talked she rocked ever so slightly forward and back as if in prayer. Her words were ginger, cinnamon, nutmeg, and thyme, but her voice was something else.

The flight hadn't seemed half over and we were being told to prepare for landing. As I packed my unread book away... "Bob, would you like a Tic Tac?"

"Why yes I would, Esther."

The candy box was in her left hand. As she reached across the empty seat between us, her sleeve inched up her forearm. There, tattooed in black were a series of numbers from a time long ago, a time without latkes.

As we departed the plane, I said, "When I get home I'll make your latkes, Esther."

"*Kaddishel*, Bob," she responded, "*Kaddishel*."

I was to learn later that a Jewish son is affectionately referred to as "my *Kaddish*," the one who will say Kaddish, the Jewish prayer for the dead, for me.

Robert Golling Jr. is a U.S. Navy veteran of the Vietnam War and a retired telephone engineer. He no longer travels on business. He does practice his culinary skills every day on his two sons.

MIKKEL AALAND

$_{\star}\,{}^{\star}\,{}_{\star}$

The White Dragon

*At the height of the Cold War, a traveler in Japan
is drawn ever deeper into a Shinto project
to forestall nuclear Armageddon.*

IN MY DREAM THAT FIRST NIGHT IN TOKYO, A MAN NAMED Kazz was behind me, and I could sense him smiling with pride. In a misty, featureless foreground I perceived four or five ghostly figures dressed in white robes. They were hurling long, vicious daggers at me. But ten feet before me, the daggers turned into dinner knives, the kind with dull, rounded tips. I easily deflected them from my body with my hands, and they fell harmlessly to the ground. I didn't feel fear or concern. Rather, I felt awkward, as if something were happening that I didn't understand—as though I were part of a game for which I didn't know the rules.

I awoke from my puzzling dream in the tiny hotel room. I didn't know what time it was. My internal body clock said midmorning, California time, but the darkness outside reminded me I was at the Asia Center Hotel in Tokyo, in the middle of the night—only a few days away from finally meeting the mysterious Kazz and his venerable teacher.

I heard Donna stir and then roll over on her side. Our

173

relationship had evolved a lot since I had told my friend Dan about her on Mount Shasta four months earlier. Not only did we share the swimming pool, art, and bed, but when I told her about the Shinto project she was intrigued.[1] She saw it as a wonderful performance piece, and the Shinto priest who had started it as an artist in his own right. All it needed, she said, was a Philip Glass score. In November, when I asked if she'd join me on a trip to Japan, she didn't hesitate. She had been fascinated with Japan for a long time, and was curious to meet the man behind the Sword of Heaven project.

It was raining lightly, typical autumn weather in central Japan. Restless, I clicked on my reading light and quietly opened my briefcase to reread the letter I had received from Kazz a few weeks earlier. His back was better, and he was once again placing gods.

"I just came back to Japan after I have placed the gods in three places, Madras, Colombo, and Mauritius Island. We have forty Gods left. My teacher is concerned. Time is short. If it is possible for you to come to Japan before the 23rd of November, please write. We have a special ceremony then."

I shook my head, placing the letter on the table. "He's right about time being short," I thought. "The world is more dangerous than ever."

I had rationalized our trip to this expensive Asian archipelago in a number of ways: a photo project, a travel story, a book promotion. But in all honesty, Kazz's invitation was all I

---

1. Shortly after the bombing of Hiroshima and Nagasaki, a Shinto priest had a vision of how to battle the evil that engulfed the world. He broke an ancient Shinto relic, a holy sword, into 108 pieces. Each piece was enclosed in stone. Followers of the priest began to place the stone gods in a protective ring around the world, completing the task just prior to 1990.

needed. I owed it to myself and the others who had placed gods through me to meet the people behind this ambitious project, even if the trip were a financial bust.

I heard Donna call out, "I'm wide awake! What time is it?"

"Four," I said, gently stroking her cheek. "Eleven in the morning California time. We've got hours until sunrise."

I hugged her and held her for a long time.

"Careful. My stomach. I knew I shouldn't have eaten the duck they served on the plane."

And then she stretched, her arms nearly touching the two walls of our tiny room.

"I can't go back to sleep," she said. "What shall we do?"

I knew from my last trip to Japan, eight years earlier, that the only place open at this hour was the Tsuki fish market. I suggested that we go there.

The streets were empty, and there was little sign of the massive human energy that transformed Tokyo from the rubble and ruin at the end of World War II into a gleaming, modern city, one of the most populous in the world. At the fish market we joined a few other blurry-eyed foreigners among the throng of Japanese fishmongers strolling around the vast indoor fifty-acre marketplace. There was every type of fish imaginable for sale, in every form: frozen, dried, or freshly cleaned. The waters surrounding the four main islands that make up Japan are fertile, but the huge tuna and whales obviously came from the far corners of the world. We passed a stand oozing the smell of fish broth.

"I'm not sure this was a good idea," Donna said, still nauseated from our in-flight meal.

By then it was 7 A.M. and the sun was rising, brightening the gray Tokyo sky. We went out into the now-crowded streets to find a bus back to our hotel.

There, Donna went for tea, while I went up to our room

to call Kazz. A woman answered the phone. In seconds Kazz was on the phone welcoming Donna and me to Japan. His voice was cheerful, but his English slow and careful.

"The ceremony is on Wednesday. I'll meet you at the station in a couple days, on Tuesday," he said. Then he gave me directions. We were to meet him south of Tokyo, three hours by the Shinkansen, or bullet train. Just hearing Kazz's voice on the phone thrilled me. There is a real person behind the letters, I thought. And I'm going to finally meet him!

It was twilight when we arrived at Kashiharajingumae, a small train station between Nara and Osaka. We were met by neon advertisements blasting messages about donuts and burgers. Into this chaotic scene walked a man wearing a jogging suit, his long black hair wild as if he had just finished a long run. He called out my name, mispronouncing it. It was Kazz.

I don't remember if we bowed. Our meeting seemed so Western, with him in a jogging suit surrounded by fast-food joints. I just grabbed his hand and shook it. After I introduced Donna, Kazz grew silent, donning an impassive Asian public countenance. He gripped our baggage and led us to his car.

"It's old," he apologized.

"What? The car?" I joked. At most it was three years old.

"The Japanese don't like used things. We were given it as a gift."

The silence returned. Donna climbed in back, and I sat on the left, where in America the driver's seat would be. In Japan the driver sits on the right, British-style. In the awkwardness of our continued silence, I wanted to grab the nonexistent wheel.

Finally Kazz broke the silence as we drove away from the station. "There is much to tell."

I was relieved. I hadn't known how to handle his silence, and I was dying to talk. "Where are we going?" I asked.

"Tonight the teacher is preparing for tomorrow's ceremony. The mountain is only an hour's drive."

What mountain? Juan never mentioned a mountain. I sensed a widening gap between Kazz and me, and I wanted to fill it with answers as fast as possible. At that moment, however, I knew intuitively that I needed to restrain myself.

"Was that your wife who answered the phone?" I asked instead.

"Yes."

"What does she think of all your travel?" Donna asked from the backseat.

"She understands." Kazz managed a smile, as he half turned to her. "Most of the time."

The small town and its neon melted into darkness behind us. We followed narrow cobblestone roads past smaller towns and villages divided by dark patches of what I assumed were rice fields. Even though we were far from the intense urban density of Tokyo, the countryside felt carefully shaped and planned out. Nothing seemed out of place, not a single cobblestone. An hour later we began climbing a steep mountain road.

"This is Mount Katsuragi. Soon we arrive at Tenkenjinja, the shrine of the Sword of Heaven," Kazz said, as he twisted the steering wheel to follow the sharp curves in the road. "The teacher is waiting."

At the mention of the teacher, I felt a childlike eagerness and impatience. My vision of him was pure fantasy, a high lama of Shangri-la, old, frail, and wrinkled. I've always loved James Hilton's *Lost Horizon,* the book that introduced Shangri-la to the world. Perhaps I'd be like Conway, the book's main character, and the teacher would reveal some marvelous secret that would change my life.

"How did you meet him?" I asked.

Maybe Kazz was deliberately trying to sustain the drama to

make our meeting more mysterious, because he didn't answer. Instead, he said simply, "Please wait."

We were silent a long time. Then Donna, bless her heart, said, "At least tell us his name." Her vision of the teacher clearly was more objective than mine. She saw him as a talented artist creating a masterpiece and therefore very human. She had her feet planted firmly on the ground while I floated in a cloud of fantasy.

Kazz gripped the steering wheel tightly. "Hakuryu Takizawa."

"Hakuryu Takizawa?" she repeated.

"Hakuryu means White Dragon. Takizawa is his family name," Kazz said. Before she could say anything more he pulled the car to the side of the road. "Here we are."

It was dark, but we could faintly see a valley far below. I saw the black outline of a crow sitting on a bare late-autumn branch. The new moon was just emerging over the hillside terraces. The darkness began to glow with a dull silver sheen.

"It's late," I said.

"No problem," replied Kazz as he opened the car door and led us down a steep path to a dimly lit house.

The man who watched us walk through the door was no frail lama. He leapt from the floor, moving quickly across the tatami mats, and put out his hand in a hearty Western-style greeting.

"Yokuirashaimashita!" he said in a deep voice, welcoming us in Japanese. He was slender and tall, approaching my own height of six feet. He was wearing a white, two-piece garment: a long skirt under a robe-length coat. His eyes were piercing. They darted between me and Donna with the happiness of a grandfather seeing his grandchildren for the first time, without the sagelike reserve that I had expected, especially after Kazz's reticence.

He greeted Donna by clasping her small hand carefully between both of his and smiling deeply at the same time.

He turned to his student and spoke rapidly in Japanese. Kazz motioned us toward the center of the room, where a kerosene heater glowed warmly. There was also a cooking pit with coals that filled the room with steam and the smell of food.

The room was large and open, and in the back, in the shadow of the kerosene heater, two figures came towards us. One was an older woman, her head bowed as she walked forward; the other was a tall young man. The teacher's wife and son offered polite greetings, and then returned to the back of the room where they had been sleeping.

"Do they live here?" I asked Kazz.

"Nobody lives here. They just stay here before ceremonies. The teacher lives nearby, in Osaka."

I was anxious to ask the teacher questions about the Sword of Heaven, but to do so at this point seemed hasty. Instead, we spent the next fifteen minutes in casual conversation, with Kazz translating.

"Do you want some broth?" the teacher asked, pointing to a black pot full of boiling liquid, unrecognizable vegetables, and glutinous rice.

I accepted and it tasted wonderful. Donna, however, declined. The teacher looked concerned, but Donna reassured him that it had nothing to do with the broth, that her stomach was upset from something she ate and she was sure it would be fine soon.

The teacher asked if I had been to Japan before, and I told him only once, when I was researching a book on bathing customs. Pleased that I had taken such an interest in one of the great passions of the Japanese people, he told us that we mustn't miss the southern island, Kyushu, where people lie on the beach and have themselves covered with sand heated by volcanic water.

When the teacher asked me how old I was, I learned that Kazz and I were the same age, thirty-one. The teacher told us that according to the Chinese calendar, we were both dragons.

"What does being a dragon mean?" I asked.

"Both of you are very stubborn," he replied with a knowing smile.

Then the teacher asked if Donna and I were married.

I told him no, we weren't married. We'd only been together for five months. I briefly wondered if our unwed intimacy would offend him, but it didn't seem to. He replied that we looked like brother and sister, which surprised me when I considered Donna's Italian background in contrast to my Nordic one. It also struck me as an odd comment, especially since I was sleeping with her. I felt a little defensive until he explained, "Your souls. You both have *yasai*, gentle souls."

Although the teacher exchanged glances with both Donna and me, his questions, including the one about us being married or not, were focused mostly toward me. Donna was content to sit back and just listen. I was confident that later, when we were alone, I could count on her as a reality-check. She'd be able to temper my judgment with more detached reasoning.

When Kazz suggested that now would be a good time to ask the teacher about the project, I sat up straight.

"First, tell the teacher that I am honored to help with his peace project, even in such a small way," I said to Kazz.

The teacher smiled and nodded when Kazz translated my English into Japanese. "But it's not my project. It is the project of God. We may think differently, but it is God who put us in contact with one another."

Kazz leaned toward the teacher and asked him to repeat something, then he turned back to me. "Are you a Christian?"

I'd never been asked that question so directly before. "I'm not involved with any organized religion," I replied.

As a child I had attended Livermore's Unitarian Church. Sunday services often meant a field trip to the Rosicrucian Museum in nearby San Jose, or to the planetarium in San Francisco's Golden Gate Park rather than a stuffy church sermon. I had always held Christianity at arm's length, but a Unitarian, I suspected, wouldn't have had any trouble with me sitting in that room, discussing and sharing religious ideas with a Shinto priest. They might even have invited the priest to come talk in their own church.

"At least I'm not involved now," I added, since I hadn't been to a Unitarian service since I was eleven or twelve years old.

"I've never had much interest in Christianity," the teacher said bluntly.

He looked carefully for my reaction. I didn't say anything, nervously scratching behind my ear.

The teacher smiled.

"Many Christian missionaries come to Japan. They talk from their head. They feel empty inside. They don't have any personal power."

Again, he looked at me carefully before continuing.

"They call themselves Christians, but they confuse me. Jesus Christ is another one of God's projects, a gift to the human world from God. He has much power."

He spoke in the present tense, and I mentioned that to Kazz.

"He met Jesus during one of our ceremonies," Kazz said casually.

I shifted my legs uncomfortably under me. "He met Jesus Christ?"

"Yes. He left his body and his spirit traveled to Tibet. That's where all the great teachers live—Buddha, Mohammed, Confucius…Christ."

I looked over at Donna, who I knew had been raised Catholic but didn't formally practice it anymore. She looked as puzzled as I felt. The teacher caught my glance, nodded and said: "Yes, I was very impressed with Jesus. He taught me about the Great Love, how God protects not only some of the people or some of the world, but gives love to all humankind."

I didn't know how to respond. I was thrown off by how casually the teacher had brought up out-of-body travel, as if it were a completely natural thing for him to do. I was also surprised that the simplest of all of Christ's messages—to love unconditionally—was a radically new concept for him. Yet I was deeply impressed that he had cut right to what I considered the essence of Christ's teachings.

"Yes," I said slowly, "There's a big difference between Christ's teachings and a lot of organized Christianity. But please don't judge all Christians by the acts of a few."

"The same with Shinto!" the teacher exclaimed. "Many people think of World War II when they think of Shinto."

The teacher settled back, putting his bowl away.

"That is such a small part of our long history, the War. Bad spirits were in control." Now he spoke softly, with heaviness in his voice. "Long ago, in the beginning, Shinto didn't even have a name. But then Buddhism, Confucianism, and Christianity came to us from the outside world. These religions had books and dogma. In response, our leaders commissioned a written chronicle of the ancient legends, which became known as the Kojiki. They also commanded a name be given to it: Shinto, or the way of the gods."

The teacher sat up. "But I am afraid that by giving it a name, we lost the original spirit of Shinto. We caged a powerful bird. During World War II, the bird became sick. Did you know what MacArthur did after he stripped the emperor of his divinity?" the teacher asked. "He outlawed the possession of swords!"

I had forgotten that detail. At that moment the thought struck me as comical.

My country had just blasted two of Japan's major cities to radioactive dust, and we were scared of swords?

"But the sword represented militarism, like the swastika in Nazi Germany," I offered, perhaps a little apologetically.

"Then, yes," said the teacher. "But the sword also represents positive action. In any case, the sword is only one symbol of Shinto. The jewel, which represents the heart, and the mirror, which represents knowledge, are others. When all three of these divine treasures—the sword, the jewel, and the mirror—are worshipped and understood, man is complete."

I asked the teacher what he did during the war. I carefully phrased the question so that he could, if he wanted, gracefully decline.

"I was in Manchuria," he replied easily. "I was a commissary clerk." I assumed that this meant he didn't see any action, or more bluntly, that he didn't kill anyone.

Then the teacher asked me, just as carefully, if I had relatives who fought in the war with Japan.

"A family friend. On my mother's side," I replied. "He was killed at Pearl Harbor."

There was an awkward silence. In all honesty, I didn't know much about the guy. I remembered only that my American grandmother once told me about visiting Hawaii and placing flowers on his grave.

After a long pause, he said, "Before, I prayed to the God of Japan. Now I never pray to the God of Japan. I pray to the God of the Universe, Ameno-Minakanushi-no-kami, or to the Sun Goddess, Amaterasu-Omikami."

At this statement, Kazz stopped translating and looked at the teacher intently.

"What?" I asked, noting his concern.

"This is a very radical idea," Kazz said finally.

"Including the rest of the world in his prayers?"

Kazz glanced at the teacher but didn't translate. He turned back to me. "The idea of placing Shinto gods beyond Japanese soil is hard for many people to understand or accept. Even within our group, only a few people know."

I pulled back, once again totally confused.

"What about the project?" I asked. "It isn't just about saving Japan, is it? It's about saving the entire world, right?"

"Of course."

At this point the teacher yawned. His wife was already asleep on a tatami mat. Donna's eyes were closing. "Soon it will be dawn," said Kazz, impassively, ignoring my troubled look. "Translating is very tiring. You can ask the teacher more questions later."

Donna and I were given separate futons and bedding, which we placed next to each other in a corner of the room. I wanted to ask Donna what she thought but she was already asleep. I lay on the cushioned floor, staring at the wooden rafters. For the moment I felt satisfied. So what if the teacher hadn't fulfilled my fantasies—at least he wasn't a religious extremist. In fact, both Kazz and the teacher seemed like sincere and reasonable people. Hey, he was open-minded enough to evoke Jesus Christ! Then I remembered the out-of body travel and the fact that the project was secret from most of the teacher's followers. Before I fell asleep, I had a strong sense that the deeper I delved into the project the less I would understand.

Mikkel Aaland is a writer, photographer, and the author of six books, including The Sword of Heaven: A Five Continent Odyssey to Save the World, *from which this story was excerpted. His work has appeared in* Wired, American Photo, *and* Outside *magazine. He lives in San Francisco with his wife and two children.*

DAVID ABRAM

* * *

Stripped Naked

Sometimes a raptor can rattle your feathers.

ALTHOUGH THE INDONESIAN ISLANDS ARE HOME TO AN astonishing diversity of birds, it was only when I went to study among the Sherpa people of the high Himalayas that I was truly initiated into the avian world. The Himalayas are young mountains, their peaks not yet rounded by the endless action of wind and ice, and so the primary dimension of the visible landscape is overwhelmingly vertical. Even in the high ridges one seldom attains a view of a distant horizon; instead one's vision is deflected upward by the steep face of the next mountain. The whole land has surged skyward in a manner still evident in the lines and furrows of the mountain walls, and this ancient dynamism readily communicates itself to the sensing body.

In such a world those who dwell and soar in the sky are the primary powers. They alone move easily in such a zone, swooping downward to become a speck near the valley floor, or spiraling into the heights on invisible currents. The wingeds, alone, carry the immediate knowledge of what is unfolding on the far side of the next ridge, and hence it is only by watching them that one can be kept apprised of climatic changes in the offing, as well as of subtle shifts in the flow and density of air currents in one's own valley. Several of the shamans that I met in Nepal had birds as their close familiars. Ravens are constant commentators on village affairs. The smaller, flocking birds perform aerobatics in unison over the village rooftops, twisting and swerving in a perfect sympathy of motion, the whole flock appearing like a magic banner that floats and flaps on air currents over the village, then descends in a heap, only to be carried aloft by the wind a moment later, rippling and swelling.

For some time I visited a Sherpa *dzankri* whose rock home was built into one of the steep mountainsides of the Khumbu region in Nepal. On one of our walks along the narrow cliff trails that wind around the mountain, the *dzankri* pointed out to me a certain boulder, jutting out from the cliff, on which he had "danced" before attempting some especially difficult cures. I recognized the boulder several days later when hiking back down toward the *dzankri's* home from the upper yak pastures, and I climbed onto the rock, not to dance but to ponder the pale white and red lichens that gave life to its surface, and to rest. Across the dry valley, two lammergeier condors floated between gleaming, snow-covered peaks. It was a ringing blue Himalayan day, clear as a bell. After a few moments I took a silver coin out of my pocket and aimlessly began a simple sleight-of-hand exercise, rolling the coin over the knuckles of my right hand. I had taken to practicing this somewhat monotonous exercise in response to the endless flicking of prayer beads by the older Sherpas, a practice usually accompanied by a repetitively chanted prayer: *"Om Mani Padme Hum"* (O the Jewel in the Lotus). But there was no prayer accompanying my revolving coin, aside from my quiet breathing and the dazzling sunlight. I noticed that one of the two condors in the distance had swerved away from its partner and was now floating over the valley, wings outstretched. As I watched it grow larger, I realized, with some delight, that it was heading in my general direction; I stopped rolling the coin and stared. Yet just then the lammergeier halted in its flight, motionless for a moment against the peaks, then swerved around and headed back toward its partner in the distance. Disappointed, I took up the coin and began rolling it along my knuckles once again, its silver surface catching the sunlight as it turned, reflecting the rays back into the sky. Instantly, the condor swung out from its path and began soaring back in a wide arc. Once again, I watched its shape grow larger. As the great size of the bird became apparent, I felt my skin begin to crawl and come alive, like a swarm of bees all in motion, and a humming grew loud in my ears. The coin continued rolling along my fingers. The creature loomed larger, and larger still, until, suddenly, it was there—an immense silhouette hovering just above my head, huge wing feathers rustling ever so slightly as they mastered the breeze. My fingers were frozen, unable to move; the coin dropped out of my hand. And then I felt myself stripped naked by an alien gaze infinitely more lucid and precise than my own. I do not know for how long I was transfixed, only that I felt the air streaming past naked knees and heard the wind whispering in my feathers long after the Visitor had departed.

David Abram is a philosopher, ecologist, and sleight-of-hand magician who has lived and traded magic with indigenous cultures on several continents. He is the author The Spell of the Sensuous: Perception and Language in a More-Than-Human World, *from which this story was excerpted.*

★ ★ ★

Encounter with a Stranger

*In South India, the author meets
a very old friend.*

THREE MONTHS LATER I FOUND MYSELF IN THE SOUTH OF India, in Pondicherry, a former French colonial town on the sea, visiting the ashram of Aurobindo. I had not heard of Aurobindo or Pondicherry before I came back to India; I had no intentions of visiting any ashrams (four years' experience at an Oxford college had cured me of any fascination with "monasticism"). I went there on a whim, on a chance remark from a fellow traveler who had found me thin and depressed in a fleapit in Tanjore and said, "Go to Pondy and get yourself a supply of good English beer, French bread, and a clean room."

My first days in Pondicherry—despite the English beer, French bread, and clean room—were disgruntled. The city it-self unnerved me with its long, straight, empty avenues baking in unwaveringly harsh sun. I disliked the ashram with its pompous colonial buildings and air of goody-goody white-washed piety. What little I gleaned of Aurobindo's philosophy of evolution struck me as ridiculous. I wrote to a friend in England who had been afraid I would "get religion" in India, that Aurobindo was obviously an escapee from reality, a fanta-sist of the most grandiose proportions. How could anyone but a fantasist believe at this moment that humankind had any hope of saving itself, let alone "leaping into Divine Being," or some such rubbish, after the Gulags, the First and Second World Wars? After Hiroshima and Auschwitz, Kampuchea and Vietnam? As for sweet Mother, his *Shakti*, the half-French half-Turkish sibyl who had accompanied him on his "adven-ture," I wrote: "I see nothing in the so-called Mother of the Universe and Co-creator of the coming transformation of human beings into divine infants but an ancient Jewess with an appalling taste in clothes." I ended the letter: "I am leaving this incense-scented morgue tomorrow for the beach (any beach anywhere) and a little sensual sanity. I'd rather die drunk in a Calcutta ditch than spend another day here."

In fact, I went on to spend four more months.

That evening I met Jean-Marc Frechette and began a friendship that would change my life.

He was standing in front of me in the ashram food queue, frail, stooped, with balding light chestnut hair and large, slightly protruding eyes, reading Jaccottet's translations of Hopkins. I was so relieved to see someone reading and not wandering in the usual ashram daze that I moved close to him and craned over his shoulder. We started talking and contin-ued most of the night. He was from Montreal and lived in a guest house near the ashram. He loved Rilke, Piero della Francesca, and Callas, as I did; we had a whole culture in common, and that bound us immediately. But he had made a transition into the Eastern world that I had not managed.

"Why are you here?" I asked him.

"To change my life."

"You believe in Aurobindo's philosophy?"

"I experience his philosophy."

That made me furious. As we walked by the sea I launched into a denunciation of the escapism of ashrams in general and the uselessness of Eastern wisdom in the face of the problems of the world.

"The world is in its last nightmare, and sweet old clichés like 'peace of mind' and 'the power of meditation' and 'evolution into divine being' aren't going to wake it up. So-called Eastern wisdom is as bankrupt and helpless as that of the West—more so, in fact, because its claims are so much more grandiloquent."

Jean-Marc heard me out with barely suppressed amusement.

"Why don't you just let go of it?" he said.

"Let go of what?"

"The toy you are holding."

"Don't be cryptic."

"You are holding on to horror and tragedy like a child on to its last toy. It is all you have left, the last rags of a costume you do not want to give up."

His certainty exploded me into another tirade. "I'd rather die than be calm. I'd rather die of the horror I see everywhere than hide from it in some snug yogic catatonia."

Jean-Marc dropped to the sand laughing.

"Oh, my god," he said, wiping his eyes. "No wonder you like Callas so much."

He imitated my indignant face and flailing arms.

"You see the world as one long grim nineteenth-century opera with nothing in it but pain and loss. You refuse to imagine anything but catastrophe."

He started laughing again. "How conventional."

"Stop laughing, damn you!"

"I don't have to stop laughing. You have to start. Don't you see how absurd you are being? Look around you. Feel this night, its sweetness, the softness of the sand where we are walking. You've been running from your spirit for years. You must stop. You must sit down, shut up, open, listen, and wait. Give your soul a chance to breathe. Never in my life have I seen a performance such as the one you have just given. The only thing you didn't do is cut open a vein."

He stood up and put his arm around me. "The room next to mine in the guest house is vacant tomorrow. Why don't you take it? We could go on talking and walking by the sea. I could introduce you to my poetic genius, and we could drink tea in the garden in the afternoon like old British colonels."

Undoing a year's careful planning, I accepted.

Jean-Marc's gift to me—for which I will always be grateful—was to live the spiritual life before my eyes with such a happy simplicity I could not deny its truth. Jean-Marc had given up all "normal" life for a small room with a badly working fan by the sea in South India. He had almost no money, no job to go to, no ring of friends to sustain his choice— nothing, in fact, but his faith, his few books of Claudel, Rene Char, and Aurobindo, and the sound of the sea. Yet he was the clearest man I had ever known, spare, joyful, delightfully eccentric, like his room with its narrow, lopsided wooden bed, its desk with one leg propped up by an old copy of the Upanishad, its cracked blue china bowl kept always full of flowers. Nothing interested him less than preaching his mystic insights; he lived them, writing them down in huge swirling letters in the garden swept by sea wind, reading Meister Eckhart and John of the Cross, swigging tea from a flask, walking up and down the beach in his loping zigzag gait, his eyes brilliant with mischief and hilarity. Jean-Marc never talked about renunciation or expiation; although he had been brought up a Quebecois Catholic in a country village, he detested all notions of guilt and original sin—"how vulgar to imagine that God cannot forgive anything," "this world is divine," he would repeat again and again, leaning down to stroke the beach like an old dog or ruffling the long grass with closed eyes. "Hopkins was right: 'There lives the dearest freshness deep down in things.' You just have to go deep enough to find it and to stay with it."

"Your problem," he would say, lowering his voice conspiratorially, "is that, like so many post-romantics, you find suffering glorious. Pain has become your substitute for religion. But pain is not glorious, it is boring. Joy is glorious. Praise is glorious. Because they are hard. You have to work at them with your whole being. Your other problem is that you want—like almost every other intellectual Westerner I have ever met—to do everything yourself. You think there is something "unmanly" in asking anyone else for help, let alone looking for a Master who could guide you. Meister Eckhart said: 'A fly in God is greater that an angel in himself.' You are a vain angel."

Slowly Jean-Marc persuaded me to go with him to the ashram, to visit Aurobindo's tomb, to examine my earlier dismissal of meditation. One day he said, "Why don't you just sit by Aurobindo's tomb and see what happens?" I sat day after day with the other silent meditators by the white slab heaped with lotuses and jasmine. Nothing happened; I just felt hot, sad, and angry at the confusion in my mind.

Then, one afternoon, just as I decided to leave and get some tea, the thoughts that had been racing through my brain were suddenly silenced. I felt my entire being gasp for joy, a kind of joy I had never before experienced. I did not tell Jean-Marc for fear that if I talked about the experience it would vanish—but it repeated with more or less the same intensity for days afterward.

At last I told him.

"Well…" Jean-Marc smiled. "Now you know that the power of meditation is not a 'sweet old cliché.' Your new life is starting."

We went to the Hôtel de Ville on the seafront and celebrated with one tepid bottle of beer each. Later, as we sat on the beach under a nearly full moon, he wrote out one of his poems for me in the sand:

> O moon
> Mingle our quiet tears
> With the tail of comets…
> For so the soul begins.

Now Jean-Marc began to lay before me the visionary treasures of his inner life. I listened astonished as he told me of a vision he had had in Duino Castle when Aurobindo had appeared to him in the middle of a lotus of fire; a week before I would have been tempted to dismiss this as fantasy, but now each detail seemed essential, a key to a new possibility.

"Mystics are not special human beings," Jean-Marc said. "Each human being is a special kind of mystic. Not everyone, however, wants to know this or to find out what it means. Those who do, and who become conscious of their inner power, see and know as clearly as you and I see this rose or the sea outside the window."

I still had no real idea what he was talking about. Experiences of the next few weeks would sweep that ignorance away.

Every day I meditated before sleep and soon began to hear a low hum coming from all around me, the walls, the flowers, the sound of the sea itself. If I tried too hard to concentrate on it, it would go away. When I let my mind rest, it would surround me. I told Jean-Marc.

"Good," he said. "So that is beginning."

I pressed him.

"Creation has a sound. You are hearing it, or part of it."

One night, about a week after I had been hearing the sound, I had the first vision of my life, which overturned everything I had known up until then.

I fell asleep but I did not feel it like sleep at all. I was simply at peace, detached from my body, which I could see lying beneath me. Rapidly, as if in a great wind, I found myself taken to a white room, open to sounds of the afternoon, in which Aurobindo himself was sitting, white-haired, calm, surrounded by a group of silent disciples. The room was not his room in Pondicherry, which I had seen, but one more ancient. I felt as if I were in ancient India. Nothing was said; I moved toward Aurobindo naturally, as if to a long-lost father. I put my head in his lap, and he rested one hand on it.

Then I entered a cloud of swirling light. The Light was filled with thousands and thousands of voices, all singing in rapture. Some of the words I could make out, some were in languages I knew, some in languages I had never heard before. I heard my own voice singing with them, mingling with theirs, singing the words, "I hate to leave you, but it is your will and I must go down." I did not know what the words meant, but my heart was filled with an immense love for the Light I was mingled with. Having to leave it filled me with grief; my voice burned and rose and fell with the others.

The music stopped. I found myself bound, almost choking, in a dark chute hurtling down what seemed like a long slide. Then, with a bump, I hit ground and woke up.

I heard the words distinctly, spoken in a calm male voice:

"Remember who you are. Remember where you come from."

My body was flooded with waves of blissful energy that swept up and down into the pulse and rhythm of the music I had heard.

As soon as I could collect myself, I went out into the morning, lay in the long grass of the garden, and wept with gratitude.

Then fear began. Was I going mad? What would I do with this new, overwhelming knowledge? How would I always remember who I am and where I came from? I knew I had been graced with a great insight, but what would I do with it?

"What do you do?" Jean-Marc laughed. "You get down on your knees and say a hundred thousand thank-yous for a start. Then you wait."

"Wait?" I exploded.

Jean-Marc broke into wild laughter. "Two weeks ago you denied enlightenment existed. Now you want to be enlightened instantly. Some people work and wait years for what you have just been given, and here you are already demanding everything. Go on meditating; be calm. And, for God's sake, enjoy yourself."

Even after my vision I avoided reading Aurobindo seriously. I had an intuition that I would have to be taught inwardly how to read him, that if I read him too soon and with an unripe, defensive, or merely curious mind, I would miss the immediacy of his vision. All my life I had thought myself intelligent enough to understand anything: now I realized how limited my understanding of intelligence had been. Nothing in my Western training could help me explore what I had begun to see; now I knew only enough to know I would have to trust and be led forward by whatever Power was educating me.

In the following weeks of quiet talks with Jean-Marc and meditation by Aurobindo's tomb, I began to see how much of my inner life my mind had been repressing or denying. A thousand memories of my Indian childhood returned in their old wide happiness: I began to connect the joys I had known in music and friendship and in a few moments of lovemaking with the greater joy that was dawning in my spirit. I began to see how my fascination with the drama of my emotional life and my too-great faith in the powers of my intellect had withered my spirit. Jean-Marc had a dream of me in black, sitting at the end of a long, dark corridor, surrounded by books. "You have become imprisoned in the knowledge you acquired in order to 'become' yourself," he said to me. "Now you must let it go so another knowledge can arrive."

About a week after the first vision I was given another one in sleep, although it was more vivid than any dream.

I was sitting on one of the beaches of my childhood, the beach at Cannanore, where I had often gone in the summer holidays with my mother. In the distance I could see fishermen on their primitive boats, and the sight of their lean, tough bodies in the sun comforted me.

Something told me to look to my right. Far down the beach a figure in white was walking in my direction. As it came closer I saw the figure had a face of blinding beauty— oval, golden with large, tender eyes. I had no idea whether the figure was male or female or both, but a love for it and a kind of high, refined desire began in me. With a shock I realized the figure was coming toward me, had, in fact, walked the length of the beach to come to me. The figure approached, sat down so close by me in the sand that I could smell its sandalwood fragrance.

I had no idea what to do. I sat with my head turned away from the figure. It said, in a soft voice, "Look at me." I turned and saw its face irradiated by a golden light that was not the light of the afternoon dancing around us on the sand but a light emanating from its eyes and skin. It put out a hand and touched my face and then cradled it.

Leaning against its breast, I experienced the most complete love for any other being I had ever felt, a love in which there was desire, but a desire so fiery and clear it filled my whole self and was focused nowhere.

Still embraced, I asked the figure, "Who are you?"

The voice came back, amused and gentle: "Who am I? Who do you think I am? I am you."

I fainted, and awoke.

Andrew Harvey is the author of A Journey to Ladakh, Burning Houses, The Web, *and* Hidden Journey: A Spiritual Awakening, *from which this story was excerpted. He was the youngest fellow ever elected to Oxford, and has written several books of poetry and works of translation.*

Recommended Reading

Aaland, Mikkel. *The Sword of Heaven: A Five Continent Odyssey to Save the World*. San Francisco: Travelers' Tales, 1999.

Abram, David. *The Spell of the Sensuous: Perception and Language in a More-than-Human World*. New York: Pantheon, 1996.

Atwater, P. M. H. *Future Memory: How Those Who "See the Future" Shed New Light on the Workings of the Human Mind*. New York: Birch Lane Press, 1996.

Aurobindo, Sri. *The Life Divine, Vol. 19*. India: Sri Aurobindo Ashram, 1970.

Bender, Sue. *Everyday Sacred: A Woman's Journey Home*. San Francisco: HarperSan Francisco, 1995.

Bernardin, Joseph Louis. *The Gift of Peace: Personal Reflections*. Chicago: Loyola Press, 1997.

Bolen, Jean Shinoda, M.D. *Crossing to Avalon: A Woman's Midlife Pilgrimage*. San Francisco: HarperSan Francisco, 1995.

Brown, Mick. *The Spiritual Tourist: A Personal Odyssey through the Outer Reaches of Belief*. New York: Bloomsbury, 1998.

Chernin, Kim. *Reinventing Eve: Modern Woman in Search of Herself*. New York: HarperPerennial, 1994; New York: Times Books, 1987.

Cooper, Rabbi David A. *Entering the Sacred Mountain: Exploring the Mystical Practices of Judaism, Buddhism, and Sufism*. New York: Bell Tower, 1994.

Covington, Dennis. *Salvation on San Mountain: Snake Handling and Redemption in Southern Appalachia.* New York: Perseus, 1995.

Cowan, James G. *Messengers of the Gods: Tribal Elders Reveal the Ancient Wisdom of the Earth.* New York: Bell Tower, 1993.

Cousineau, Phil. *The Art of Pilgrimage: The Seeker's Guide to Making Travel Sacred.* Berkeley: Conari Press, 1998.

Davies, Paul. God and the New Physics. New York: Simon & Schuster, 1983.

Deming, Alison Hawthorne. *Temporary Homelands: Essays on Nature, Spirit and Place.* New York: Picador, 1996.

Dossey, Larry, M.D. *Recovering the Soul.* New York: Bantam Books, 1989.

Ehrlich, Gretel. *Questions of Heaven: The Chinese Journeys of an American Buddhist.* Boston: Beacon Press, 1997.

Eliade, Mircea, ed. *The Encyclopedia of Religion, Vol. 13.* New York: Macmillan, 1987.

Elliott, William. *Tying Rocks to Clouds: Meetings and Conversations with Wise and Spiritual People.* Wheaton, Illinois: Quest Books, 1995.

Frankl, Viktor. *Man's Search for Meaning.* Seattle: University of Washington Press, 1959.

Gallagher, Nora. *Things Seen and Unseen: A Year Lived in Faith.* New York: Vintage, 1999.

Gallup, George, Jr. *Adventures in Immortality.* New York: McGraw-Hill, 1982

Goldberg, Natalie. *Long Quiet Highway: Waking Up in America.* New York: Bantam, 1993.

Gonzalez-Crussi, F. *Suspended Animation: Six Essays on the Preservation of Bodily Parts.* Orlando: Harvest, 1995.

Gruber, Mark, O.S.B. *Wounded by Love: Intimations of an Outpouring Heart.* Latrobe, Pennsylvania: Saint Vincent Archabbey, 1993.

Halliburton, Richard. *The Royal Road to Romance*. San Francisco: Travelers' Tales, 2001.

Harvey, Andrew. *Hidden Journey: A Hidden Awakening*. New York: Arkana, 1991.

Hogan, Linda. *Dwellings: A Spiritual History of the Living World*. New York: Touchstone, 1995.

Housden, Roger. *Sacred Journeys in a Modern World*. New York: Simon & Schuster, 1998.

Houston, James D. *In the Ring of Fire: A Pacific Basin Journey*. San Francisco: Mercury House, 1997.

Huxley, Aldous. *The Doors of Perception*. New York: Colophon Books, 1954.

Jung, C. G. *Man and His Symbols*. New York: Doubleday, 1964.

Kaku, Michio. *Hyperspace*. New York: Anchor Doubleday, 1994.

Kingsolver, Barbara. *High Tide in Tucson: Essays from Now or Never*. New York: HarperPerennial, 1995.

Kubler-Ross, Elisabeth. *On Death and Dying*. New York: Simon & Schuster Inc., 1997.

Lamott, Anne. *Traveling Mercies: Some Thoughts on Faith*. New York: Pantheon, 1999.

Lane, Belden C. *The Solace of Fierce Landscapes: Exploring Desert and Mountain Spirituality*. New York: Oxford University Press, 1998.

Lash, Jennifer. *On Pilgrimage: A Time to Seek*. London: Bloomsbury Publishing, 1991.

Lewis, C. S. *A Grief Observed*. New York: Bantam Books, 1983.

Lindbergh, Anne Morrow. *Gift from the Sea*. New York: Pantheon, 1992.

Livingston, Patricia H. *Lessons of the Heart: Celebrating the Rhythms of Life*. Notre Dame, Ind.: Ave Maria Press, 1992.

Matousek, Mark. *Sex, Death, Enlightenment: A True Story*. New York: Riverhead Books, 1996.

Matthiessen, Peter. *The Tree Where Man Was Born*. New York:
    Penguin, 1995.

Mayorga, Nancy Pope. *The Hunger of the Soul: A Spiritual
    Diary*. Studio City, Calif.: Vedanta, 1981.

Morris, Jan. *Pleasures of a Tangled Life*. New York: Random
    House, 1989.

Morton, H. V. *In the Steps of the Master*. New York: Dodd,
    Mead & Company, 1934.

Nicholl, Charles. *Borderlines: A Journey in Thailand and Burma*.
    New York: Penguin, 1988.

Norris, Kathleen. *The Cloister Walk*. New York: Riverhead
    Books, 1997.

Norris, Kathleen. *Dakota: A Spiritual Geography*. New York:
    Houghton Mifflin, 1993.

Olsen, W. Scott, and Scott Cairns, eds. *The Sacred Place:
    Witnessing the Holy in the Physical World*. Salt Lake City:
    University of Utah Press, 1996.

Remen, Rachel Naomi, M.D. *Kitchen Table Wisdom: Stories
    That Heal*. New York: Riverhead Books, 1996.

Rinpoche, Sogyal, Patrick Gaffney and Andrew Harvey
    (eds.). *The Tibetan Book of Living and Dying*. San Francisco:
    HarperSan Francisco, 1992.

Roberts, Paul William. *Empire of the Soul: Some Journeys in
    India*. New York: Riverhead Books, 1996.

Shrady, Nicholas. *Sacred Roads: Adventures from the Pilgrimage
    Trail*. San Francisco: HarperSan Francisco, 1999.

Somé, Malidoma Patrice. *Of Water and the Spirit: Ritual,
    Magic, and Initiation in the Life on an African Shaman*. New
    York: Jeremy P. Tarcher, 1994.

Talbot, Michael. *The Holographic Universe*. New York:
    HarperCollins, 1992.

Tipler, Frank J. *The Physics of Immortality*. New York:
    Doubleday, 1994.

Tóibín, Colm. *The Sign of the Cross: Travels in Catholic Europe.* London: Random House UK, 1994.

Wesselman, Hank. *Spiritwalker: Messages from the Future.* New York: Bantam, 1995.

Wolf, Fred Allen. *Star Wave: Mind, Consciousness, and Quantum Physics.* New York: Macmillan, 1984.

Wolfe, Michael. *The Hadj: An American's Pilgrimage to Mecca.* New York: Grove Press, 1993.

Yeadon, David. *The Way of the Wanderer: Discover Your True Self Through Travel.* San Francisco: Travelers' Tales, 2001.

Acknowledgments

We would like to thank our family and friends for their usual for-bearance while we put a book together. Thanks also to Larry Habegger, Tim O'Reilly, Susan Brady, Natanya Pearlman, Tara Weaver, Kathy Meengs, Krista Holmstrom, Christine Nielsen, Desiree Earl, Cynthia Lamb, Michele Wetherbee, and Judy Johnson for their support and contributions to the book. Further thanks to Dennis Helming for his assistance on this project.

"Awakening the Stone" by Kim Chernin excerpted from *Reinventing Eve: Modern Woman in Search of Herself* by Kim Chernin. Copyright © 1987 by Kim Chernin. Reprinted by permission of Stanford J. Greenburger Associates.

"We Shall Live Again" by David Yeadon excerpted from *The Way of the Wanderer: Discover Your True Self Through Travel* by David Yeadon. Copyright © 2001 by David Yeadon. Reprinted by permission of Travelers' Tales, Inc.

"Bola's Gift" by Alison Wright published with permission from the author. Copyright © 2002 by Alison Wright.

"Searching for the Good Spirit" by Leo W. Banks reprinted from the March 1999 issue of *Arizona Highways*. Copyright © by 1999 by Leo W. Banks. Reprinted by permission of the author.

"Ego te Absolvo" by Larry R. Moffitt published with permission from the author. Copyright © 2002 by Larry R. Moffitt.

"Passing Through" by Marianne Dresser excerpted from *The Road Within: True Stories of Transformation and the Soul,* edited by James O'Reilly, Sean O'Reilly and Tim O'Reilly. Copyright © 1997 by Marianne Dresser. Reprinted by permission of the author.

"Walking the Kerry Way" by Tim O'Reilly reprinted from *Travelers' Tales Ireland,* edited by James O'Reilly, Larry Habegger and Sean O'Reilly. Copyright © 2000 by Tim O'Reilly. Reprinted by permission of the author.

About the Editors

James O'Reilly, president and co-publisher of Travelers' Tales, wrote mystery serials before becoming a travel writer in the early 1980s. He's visited more than forty countries, along the way meditating with monks in Tibet, participating in West African voodoo rituals, and hanging out the laundry with nuns in Florence. He travels extensively with his wife Wenda and their three daughters. They live in Palo Alto, California.

Sean O'Reilly is a former seminarian, stockbroker, and prison instructor who lives in Arizona with his wife Brenda and their six children. He's had a life-long interest in philosophy and theology, and has recently published a book called *How to Manage Your DICK: Redirect Sexual Energy and Discover Your More Spiritually Enlightened, Evolved Self.* Widely traveled, Sean most recently completed an 18,000-mile van journey around the United States, sharing the treasures of the open road with his family. He is editor-at-large and director of international sales for Travelers' Tales.

TRAVELERS' TALES

THE SOUL OF TRAVEL

Footsteps Series

THE FIRE NEVER DIES
One Man's Raucous Romp
Down the Road of Food,
Passion, and Adventure
By Richard Sterling
ISBN 1-885-211-70-8
$14.95
"Sterling's writing is like spit-
fire, foursquare and jazzy with crackle...."
—*Kirkus Reviews*

LAST TROUT IN VENICE
The Far-Flung Escapades
of an Accidental
Adventurer
By Doug Lansky
ISBN 1-885-211-63-5
$14.95

"Traveling with Doug Lansky might result in
a considerably shortened life expectancy...but
what a way to go." —Tony Wheeler,
Lonely Planet Publications

ONE YEAR OFF
Leaving It All Behind for a
Round-the-World Journey
with Our Children
By David Elliot Cohen
ISBN 1-885-211-65-1
$14.95
A once-in-a-lifetime
adventure generously shared.

THE WAY OF THE WANDERER
Discover Your True Self
Through Travel
By David Yeadon
ISBN 1-885-211-60-0
$14.95

Experience transformation through travel
with this delightful, illustrated collection by
award-winning author David Yeadon.

TAKE ME WITH YOU
A Round-the-World
Journey to Invite a
Stranger Home
By Brad Newsham
ISBN 1-885-211-51-1
$24.00 (cloth)
"Newsham is an ideal guide. His journey, at
heart, is into humanity." —Pico Iyer, author
of *Video Night in Kathmandu*

KITE STRINGS OF THE SOUTHERN CROSS
A Woman's
Travel Odyssey
By Laurie Gough
ISBN 1-885-211-54-6
$14.95 —★★★—

ForeWord Silver Medal Winner
—*Travel Book of the Year*

THE SWORD OF HEAVEN
A Five Continent Odyssey
to Save the World
By Mikkel Aaland
ISBN 1-885-211-44-9
$24.00 (cloth)
"Few books capture the soul
of the road like *The Sword of Heaven*,
a sharp-edged, beautifully rendered memoir
that will inspire anyone." —Phil Cousineau,
author of *The Art of Pilgrimage*

STORM
A Motorcycle Journey
of Love, Endurance,
and Transformation
By Allen Noren
ISBN 1-885-211-45-7
$24.00 (cloth) —★★★—

ForeWord Gold Medal Winner
—*Travel Book of the Year*

Travelers' Tales Classics

COAST TO COAST
A Journey Across 1950s America
By Jan Morris
ISBN 1-885-211-79-1
$16.95

After reporting on the first Everest ascent in 1953, Morris spent a year journeying by car, train, ship, and aircraft across the United States. In her brilliant prose, Morris records with exuberance and curiosity a time of innocence in the U.S.

TRADER HORN
A Young Man's Astounding Adventures in 19th Century Equatorial Africa
By Alfred Aloysius Horn
ISBN 1-885-211-81-3
$16.95

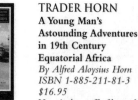

Here is the stuff of legends —tale of thrills and danger, wild beasts, serpents, and savages. An unforgettable and vivid portrait of a vanished late-19th century Africa.

THE ROYAL ROAD TO ROMANCE
By Richard Halliburton
ISBN 1-885-211-53-8
$14.95

"Laughing at hardships, dreaming of beauty, ardent for adventure, Halliburton has managed to sing into the pages of this glorious book his own exultant spirit of youth and freedom."
— *Chicago Post*

UNBEATEN TRACKS IN JAPAN
By Isabella L. Bird
ISBN 1-885-211-57-0
$14.95

Isabella Bird was one of the most adventurous women travelers of the 19th century with journeys to Tibet, Canada, Korea, Turkey, Hawaii, and Japan. A fascinating read for anyone interested in women's travel, spirituality, and Asian culture.

THE RIVERS RAN EAST
By Leonard Clark
ISBN 1-885-211-66-X
$16.95

Clark is the original Indiana Jones, relaying a breathtaking account of his search for the legendary El Dorado gold in the Amazon.

Travel Humor

NOT SO FUNNY WHEN IT HAPPENED
The Best of Travel Humor and Misadventure
Edited by Tim Cahill
ISBN 1-885-211-55-4
$12.95

Laugh with Bill Bryson, Dave Barry, Anne Lamott, Adair Lara, and many more.

THERE'S NO TOILET PAPER...ON THE ROAD LESS TRAVELED
The Best of Travel Humor and Misadventure
Edited by Doug Lansky
ISBN 1-885-211-27-9
$12.95

—★ ★ ★—
Humor Book of the Year
—Independent Publisher's Book Award

—★ ★ ★—
ForeWord Gold Medal Winner— Humor Book of the Year

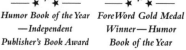

LAST TROUT IN VENICE
The Far-Flung Escapades of an Accidental Adventurer
By Doug Lansky
ISBN 1-885-211-63-5
$14.95

"Traveling with Doug Lansky might result in a considerably shortened life expectancy...but what a way to go."
—Tony Wheeler, Lonely Planet Publications

Women's Travel

A WOMAN'S PASSION FOR TRAVEL
More True Stories from A Woman's World
Edited by Marybeth Bond & Pamela Michael
ISBN 1-885-211-36-8
$17.95

"A diverse and gripping series of stories!" —Arlene Blum, author of *Annapurna: A Woman's Place*

A WOMAN'S WORLD
True Stories of Life on the Road
Edited by Marybeth Bond
Introduction by Dervla Murphy
ISBN 1-885-211-06-6
$17.95

— ★ ★ ★ —

Winner of the Lowell Thomas Award for Best Travel Book— Society of American Travel Writers

WOMEN IN THE WILD
True Stories of Adventure and Connection
Edited by Lucy McCauley
ISBN 1-885-211-21-X
$17.95

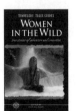

"A spiritual, moving, and totally female book to take you around the world and back." —*Mademoiselle*

A MOTHER'S WORLD
Journeys of the Heart
Edited by Marybeth Bond & Pamela Michael
ISBN 1-885-211-26-0
$14.95

"These stories remind us that motherhood is one of the great unifying forces in the world" —*San Francisco Examiner*

Food

ADVENTURES IN WINE
True Stories of Vineyards and Vintages around the World
Edited by Thom Elkjer
ISBN 1-885-211-80-5
$17.95

Humanity, community, and brotherhood comprise the marvelous virtues of the wine world. This collection toasts the warmth and wonders of this large, extended family in stories by travelers who are wine novices and experts alike.

FOOD (Updated)
A Taste of the Road
Edited by Richard Sterling
Introduction by Margo True
ISBN 1-885-211-77-5
$18.95

— ★ ★ ★ —

Silver Medal Winner of the Lowell Thomas Award for Best Travel Book— Society of American Travel Writers

HER FORK IN THE ROAD
Women Celebrate Food and Travel
Edited by Lisa Bach
ISBN 1-885-211-71-6
$16.95

A savory sampling of stories by some of the best writers in and out of the food and travel fields.

THE ADVENTURE OF FOOD
True Stories of Eating Everything
Edited by Richard Sterling
ISBN 1-885-211-37-6
$17.95

"These stories are bound to whet appetites for more than food."

—*Publishers Weekly*

Spiritual Travel

THE SPIRITUAL GIFTS OF TRAVEL
The Best of Travelers' Tales
Edited by James O'Reilly and Sean O'Reilly
ISBN 1-885-211-69-4
$16.95

A collection of favorite stories of transformation on the road from our award-winning Travelers' Tales series that shows the myriad ways travel indelibly alters our inner landscapes.

THE WAY OF THE WANDERER
Discover Your True Self Through Travel
By David Yeadon
ISBN 1-885-211-60-0
$14.95

Experience transformation through travel with this delightful, illustrated collection by award-winning author David Yeadon.

PILGRIMAGE
Adventures of the Spirit
Edited by Sean O'Reilly & James O'Reilly
Introduction by Phil Cousineau
ISBN 1-885-211-56-2
$16.95

——— ★*★ ———

ForeWord Silver Medal Winner
— Travel Book of the Year

A WOMAN'S PATH
Women's Best Spiritual Travel Writing
Edited by Lucy McCauley, Amy G. Carlson & Jennifer Leo
ISBN 1-885-211-48-1
$16.95

"A sensitive exploration of women's lives that have been unexpectedly and spiritually touched by travel experiences.... Highly recommended."
— Library Journal

THE ROAD WITHIN
True Stories of Transformation and the Soul
Edited by Sean O'Reilly, James O'Reilly & Tim O'Reilly
ISBN 1-885-211-19-8
$17.95

——— ★*★ ———

Best Spiritual Book — Independent Publisher's Book Award

THE ULTIMATE JOURNEY
Inspiring Stories of Living and Dying
James O'Reilly, Sean O'Reilly & Richard Sterling
ISBN 1-885-211-38-4
$17.95

"A glorious collection of writings about the ultimate adventure. A book to keep by one's bedside—and close to one's heart." —Philip Zaleski, editor, *The Best Spiritual Writing series*

Adventure

TESTOSTERONE PLANET
True Stories from a Man's World
Edited by Sean O'Reilly, Larry Habegger & James O'Reilly
ISBN 1-885-211-43-0
$17.95

Thrills and laughter with some of today's best writers: Sebastian Junger, Tim Cahill, Bill Bryson, and Jon Krakauer.

DANGER!
True Stories of Trouble and Survival
Edited by James O'Reilly, Larry Habegger & Sean O'Reilly
ISBN 1-885-211-32-5
$17.95

"Exciting...for those who enjoy living on the edge or prefer to read the survival stories of others, this is a good pick."
— Library Journal

Special Interest

365 TRAVEL
**A Daily Book of
Journeys, Meditations,
and Adventures**
Edited by Lisa Bach
ISBN 1-885-211-67-8
$14.95

An illuminating collection
of travel wisdom and
adventures that reminds us
all of the lessons we learn while on the road.

THE GIFT
OF RIVERS
**True Stories of
Life on the Water**
*Edited by Pamela Michael
Introduction by Robert Hass*
ISBN 1-885-211-42-2
$14.95

"*The Gift of Rivers* is a
soulful compendium of wonderful stories that
illuminate, educate, inspire, and delight."
—David Brower, Chairman of
Earth Island Institute

FAMILY TRAVEL
**The Farther You Go,
the Closer You Get**
Edited by Laura Manske
ISBN 1-885-211-33-3
$17.95

"This is family travel at its
finest." —*Working Mother*

LOVE & ROMANCE
**True Stories of
Passion on the Road**
*Edited by Judith Babcock
Wylie*
ISBN 1-885-211-18-X
$17.95

"A wonderful book to
read by a crackling fire."
—*Romantic Traveling*

THE GIFT
OF BIRDS
**True Encounters
with Avian Spirits**
*Edited by Larry Habegger
& Amy G. Carlson*
ISBN 1-885-211-41-4
$17.95

"These are all wonderful,
entertaining stories offering
a *bird's-eye view!* of our avian friends."
—*Booklist*

A DOG'S WORLD
**True Stories of
Man's Best Friend
on the Road**
*Edited by Christine
Hunsicker*
ISBN 1-885-211-23-6
$12.95

This extraordinary
collection includes stories
by John Steinbeck, Helen Thayer, James
Herriot, Pico Iyer, and many others.

THE GIFT OF TRAVEL
The Best of Travelers' Tales
*Edited by Larry Habegger, James O'Reilly
& Sean O'Reilly*
ISBN 1-885-211-25-2
$14.95

"Like gourmet chefs in a French market, the
editors of Travelers' Tales pick, sift, and prod
their way through the weighty shelves of contemporary travel writing, creaming off the
very best."
—William Dalrymple, author of *City of Djinns*

Travel Advice

SHITTING PRETTY
How to Stay Clean and Healthy While Traveling
By Dr. Jane Wilson-Howarth
ISBN 1-885-211-47-3
$12.95

A light-hearted book about a serious subject for millions of travelers— staying healthy on the road—written by international health expert, Dr. Jane Wilson-Howarth.

THE FEARLESS SHOPPER
How to Get the Best Deals on the Planet
By Kathy Borrus
ISBN 1-885-211-39-2
$14.95

"Anyone who reads *The Fearless Shopper* will come away a smarter, more responsible shopper and a more curious, culturally attuned traveler."
—Jo Mancuso, *The Shopologist*

GUTSY WOMEN
More Travel Tips and Wisdom for the Road
By Marybeth Bond
ISBN 1-885-211-61-9
$12.95

Second Edition—Packed with funny, instructive, and inspiring advice for women heading out to see the world.

SAFETY AND SECURITY FOR WOMEN WHO TRAVEL
By Sheila Swan & Peter Laufer
ISBN 1-885-211-29-5
$12.95

A must for every woman traveler!

THE FEARLESS DINER
Travel Tips and Wisdom for Eating around the World
By Richard Sterling
ISBN 1-885-211-22-8
$7.95

Combines practical advice on foodstuffs, habits, and etiquette, with hilarious accounts of others' eating adventures.

THE PENNY PINCHER'S PASSPORT TO LUXURY TRAVEL
The Art of Cultivating Preferred Customer Status
By Joel L. Widzer
ISBN 1-885-211-31-7
$12.95

Proven techniques on how to travel first class at discount prices, even if you're not a frequent flyer.

GUTSY MAMAS
Travel Tips and Wisdom for Mothers on the Road
By Marybeth Bond
ISBN 1-885-211-20-1
$7.95

A delightful guide for mothers traveling with their children— or without them!

Destination Titles:
True Stories of Life on the Road

AMERICA
Edited by Fred Setterberg
ISBN 1-885-211-28-7
$19.95

FRANCE (Updated)
Edited by James O'Reilly,
Larry Habegger &
Sean O'Reilly
ISBN 1-885-211-73-2
$18.95

**AMERICAN
SOUTHWEST**
Edited by Sean O'Reilly
& James O'Reilly
ISBN 1-885-211-58-9
$17.95

GRAND CANYON
Edited by Sean O'Reilly,
James O'Reilly &
Larry Habegger
ISBN 1-885-211-34-1
$17.95

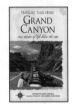

AUSTRALIA
Edited by Larry Habegger
ISBN 1-885-211-40-6
$17.95

GREECE
Edited by Larry Habegger,
Sean O'Reilly &
Brian Alexander
ISBN 1-885-211-52-X
$17.95

BRAZIL
Edited by Annette Haddad
& Scott Doggett
Introduction by Alex
Shoumatoff
ISBN 1-885-211-11-2
$17.95

HAWAI'I
Edited by Rick &
Marcie Carroll
ISBN 1-885-211-35-X
$17.95

CENTRAL AMERICA
Edited by Larry Habegger
& Natanya Pearlman
ISBN 1-885-211-74-0
$17.95

HONG KONG
Edited by James O'Reilly,
Larry Habegger &
Sean O'Reilly
ISBN 1-885-211-03-1
$17.95

CUBA
Edited by Tom Miller
ISBN 1-885-211-62-7
$17.95

INDIA
Edited by James O'Reilly
& Larry Habegger
ISBN 1-885-211-01-5
$17.95

IRELAND
Edited by James O'Reilly,
Larry Habegger &
Sean O'Reilly
ISBN 1-885-211-46-5
$17.95

SAN FRANCISCO
Edited by James O'Reilly,
Larry Habegger &
Sean O'Reilly
ISBN 1-885-211-08-2
$17.95

ITALY (Updated)
Edited by Anne Calcagno
Introduction by Jan Morris
ISBN 1-885-211-72-4
$18.95

SPAIN (Updated)
Edited by Lucy McCauley
ISBN 1-885-211-78-3
$19.95

JAPAN
Edited by Donald W. George
& Amy G. Carlson
ISBN 1-885-211-04-X
$17.95

THAILAND (Updated)
Edited by James O'Reilly
& Larry Habegger
ISBN 1-885-211-75-9
$18.95

MEXICO (Updated)
Edited by James O'Reilly
& Larry Habegger
ISBN 1-885-211-59-7
$17.95

TIBET
Edited by James O'Reilly,
Larry Habegger, & Kim
Morris
ISBN 1-885-211-76-7
$18.95

NEPAL
Edited by Rajendra
S. Khadka
ISBN 1-885-211-14-7
$17.95

TUSCANY
Edited by James O'Reilly, &
Tara Austen Weaver
ISBN 1-885-211-68-6
$16.95

PARIS
Edited by James O'Reilly,
Larry Habegger &
Sean O'Reilly
ISBN 1-885-211-10-4
$17.95